"Everyone sees what you appear to be, few really know what you are."

– Niccolò Machiavelli

Leadership, Propaganda and Democracy:
A Study of Manipulation in the Modern Presidency

2nd printing 2016

Copyright © 1996, 2016 by Trent Cotney

ISBN 978-1540382320

Preface

In 1995, this project began with the basic idea of exploring power politics in democracy. Through researching the works of Niccolò Machiavelli and Harold Lasswell, I became familiar with the use of persuasion and propaganda in the current political system. After continuing my research, I developed several typologies to categorize propaganda. I then turned to the modern presidency for examples to illustrate my theories.

Although there are many topics which arose in the course of my study, the scope of this thesis was limited to studying propaganda (no other forms of persuasion), in the modern presidency (from Theodore Roosevelt to William J. Clinton) and then applying it to Robert A. Dahl's pluralist polyarchy theory of democracy. I realize that there are many topics which were not discussed in this paper, such as public opinion and other forms of leadership or persuasion, but by limiting the research to the aforementioned topics, I was able to prepare a more concise and less ambiguous study.

This is a theory-based book. Although I do discuss the modern presidency and other historical facts, they are used only to buttress the theoretical arguments made. Three theorists, Niccolò Machiavelli, Harold D. Lasswell, and Jaques Ellul, have molded my thoughts on these topics and will be referred to throughout the book. The theories which emerge are primarily based on ideas about propaganda. Chapter One presents a typology of propaganda based on its function, use, and purpose.

These categories are separated into these group headings for two reasons. First, it allows the reader to make distinctions between the various forms. Second, although combinations and overlapping of propaganda types are possible such as positive-selective or negative-symbolic, the categories reduce ambiguities. It must also be noted that the propaganda, as I use it throughout the paper, is a morally neutral term. It should be considered neither good nor evil but merely a part of the political system.

Table of Contents

Chapter One:

Introduction

> *"In power I look only at one thing, what does it belong to and what does it effect."*

> -- Plato, The Republic

Political science is the study of power and its various relationships. Among other things, it seeks to understand the methods used by individuals to obtain and maintain power.[1] The focus of political science as both science and art is, therefore, the successes and not the failures in this quest for power. In other words, most theorists are concerned with "the study of influence and the influential."[2]

How is this influence defined? The criteria for judging power or political strength has varied over the years. In the past, power was based on a warrior's might or hunter's prowess. An individual's strength or merit was a primary determining factor in deciding who would lead. The modern day political environment, however, has shifted radically, in

---

[1] As James Madison suggests, "men are instruments of their desires...one such desire is power." Robert A. Dahl. *A Preface to Democratic Theory*, (Chicago: University of Chicago Press, 1956) 6-8.

[2] Harold D. Lasswell, *Politics: Who Gets What, When, How*, (Cleveland: Meridian Books, 1958) 13.

that, persuasion and rhetoric have now entered the forefront of politics.

Richard E. Neustadt in *Presidential Power* acknowledges the importance of the use of persuasion by leaders. In his study of American Presidents, he argues that "presidential power is the power to persuade."[3] Neustadt suggests that personal attributes and merit, in and of themselves, will not incite people to action. The President's role is, therefore, to:

> convince...men that what the White House wants of them is what they ought to do for their sake and on their authority...Presidential 'powers' may be inconclusive when a President commands, but always remain relevant as he persuades. The status and authority inherent in his office reinforce his logic and his charm.[4]

Because of the institutional limits placed on the executive branch, the President "must rely on persuasion"[5] to get things accomplished.[6]

What is persuasion? As James E. Combs and Dan Nimmo suggests, persuasion is the "propagation by the direct planting of the seed in selected soil."[7] In other words, it is any attempt to sway the opinions of others. Many

---

[3] Richard E. Neustadt, *Presidential Power*, (New York: John Wiley and Sons, Inc., 1960) 32.

[4] Ibid, 34.

[5] George Edwards, *The Public Presidency: The Pursuit of Popular Support*, (New York: New York University Press, 1983) 9.

[6] *See also* Craig Allen Smith and Kathy B. Smith, *The White House Speaks*, (Westport: Praeger, 1994) 9; Theodore J. Lowi, *The Personal President: Power Invested, Promise Unfulfilled*, (Ithaca: Cornell University Press, 1985); Jeffery K. Tulis, *The Rhetorical Presidency*, (Princeton: Princeton University Press, 1987).

[7] James E. Combs and Dan Nimmo, *The New Propaganda*, (New York: Longman, 1993) 11.

researchers have chosen to define persuasion based on its different forms. Walter F. Murphy, for example, suggests that there are five primary styles. An individual may "try by force of his intellect and will to convince" others.[8] One can attempt to sway the opinions of others by using either (2) fear or (3) affection. A fourth option involves compromise, and finally, action can be taken which would assure the individual of success.[9]

Robert A. Dahl limits his forms of persuasion to two primary types -- rational and manipulative. Rational persuasion involves appeals to logic using facts to influence opinions. It includes "a successful effort by A to enable B to come to an understanding of the true situation by means of truthful information."[10] The second form, manipulative persuasion, uses "deliberately deceptive" tactics to obtain a desired goal.[11]

Although in the greater context of their work, both Murphy and Dahl's forms of persuasion are useful, they do not encompass all of the possibilities of the term. Persuasion can be accomplished by appealing to logic, using facts, statistics, and the like, or its user can seek to manipulate the emotions of others. It may be blatant or hidden in symbols. In whatever form it may take, persuasion can be defined as any attempt to sway, induce, or urge another to act in a certain manner. In this paper, there is one type of persuasion in particular which I will explore -- propaganda.

What is propaganda? It has been defined in various ways from Edward L. Bernays' "The conscious and intelligent manipulation of the organized habits and opinions

---

[8] Walter F. Murphy, *Elements of Judicial Strategy*, (Chicago: University of Chicago Press, 1964) 40.

[9] Ibid, 40.

[10] Robert A. Dahl, *Modern Political Analysis*, (Englewood Cliffs: Prentice Hall, 1991) 40.

[11] Ibid, 40

of the masses,"[12] to Leonard W. Doob's "an attempt to modify personalities and control the behavior of individuals in relation to goals considered non-scientific or of doubtful value in a specific society and time period."[13] Propaganda, as I will be dealing with it, is a methodical attempt to purposely manipulate the values, beliefs, or actions of others. It involves the use of various techniques such as the use of advertising, speeches, or campaigns. As a form of persuasion, it can appeal to either logic or emotions.

When discussing propaganda, there are three primary questions which come to mind -- "How does it function?", "In what manner is it used?" and finally, "What does it hope to accomplish?". In order to accurately answer these questions, one must first examine the theory behind propaganda. In chapter two, I will explicate the ideas of three theorists which have influenced my approach to the study of propaganda -- Niccolò Machiavelli, Harold D. Lasswell, and Jaques Ellul.

The third chapter will examine the question: "How does propaganda function?" In this section, it will be argued that propaganda is used by the modern day Presidents to manipulate the satisfaction level in individuals to incite action.[14] In dealing with propaganda, the satisfaction level can include the public's view of their social environment, the government, or even an individual. Satisfaction in all of

---

[12] Edward L. Bernays, *Propaganda*, (New York: Horace Liveright, 1928) 9.

[13] Leonard W. Doob, *Propaganda: Its Psychology and Technique*, (New York: Henry Holt and Co., 1935) taken from Jaques Ellul, *Propaganda: The Formation of Men's Attitudes*, (New York, Alfred A. Knopf, 1965) xii.

[14] This study is confined to the modern day Presidents through 1996, that is, from Theodore Roosevelt to William Clinton. Some would argue that the modern presidency began with Franklin Roosevelt, but I will begin with Theodore Roosevelt based on the comments of other researchers -- "The two Roosevelts and Wilson shaped the modern Presidency..." Erwin C. Hargrove, *Presidential Leadership: Personality and Political Style*, (New York: Macmillan Publishing Co., Inc., 1966) 7.

these cases is directly tied to a person's happiness or his/her feelings of stability within the political system.

Categorization of Propaganda – Fig. 1.1

Function	Means	Purpose
Positive	Symbolic	Transactional
Negative	Selective	Transforming
Satisficing	Stereotyping	
	Visionary	

There are three primary categories dealing with propaganda's function -- positive, negative, and satisficing (see fig 1.1). Positive propaganda appeals to emotions such as love, hope, pride, and happiness. It can be uplifting and unifying and seek to increase the satisfaction level within individuals. Negative propaganda involves the use of negative emotive values such as anxiety, fear, anger, and the like. It is the propaganda of war, rebellions, and protests. It encompasses the general negative connotations associated with propaganda and increases or creates dissatisfaction towards an activity or group. The third category, satisficing propaganda, was developed from Herbert A. Simon's use of the word in his various works.[15] Propaganda, when used to satisfice, is designed to keep the populace content with the status quo. It does not directly seek to increase or decrease the satisfaction level but to maintain the present state.

Chapter four will discuss the means by which Presidents use propaganda. The President can use one or a combination of several distinct types of propaganda -- symbolic, selective, stereotyping, and visionary (see fig.

---

[15] *See* Herbert A. Simon's *Organizations or Models of Man* as well as his article in *Psychological Review*, vol. 63, no. 2, 1956, 129-138.

1.1). In order to answer the question: "In what manner is propaganda used?", the categories will be explored using examples from the modern day Presidents as evidence. Three things must be noted about the use of these types of propaganda. First, the key element which is being manipulated are the values of the individual.[16] Each style seeks to either reaffirm or create these values or beliefs. Second, I am fully aware that propaganda may be positive for one group and negative for another, and for this reason, I will be discussing all uses of propaganda from the President's perspective only. Finally, the categories mentioned are not isolated. It is possible to have the simultaneous use of several types of propaganda. The groupings are, however, dissimilar enough to not only be beneficial in illustrating the uses of the various forms by the Presidents, but also to show the effects of the propaganda on the sociological or ideological values of the people.

Symbolic propaganda involves an appeal to ideological or sociological values in an extremely vague manner. It is simplistic in nature, and there is no attempt to define a specific value or re-define it. Examples include holiday speeches, Presidents' waving the flag or any symbolic gesture that involves all-American values, from the President showing interest in a baseball game to kissing babies before election time.

Selective propaganda involves the selective interpretation of one or more sociological or ideological values to persuade. It calls on certain values or group of values (fiscal responsibility, law and order, equality, justice, etc.) to manipulate the masses. But, while calling on one group of values or beliefs, it naturally down plays other values. At the core of selective propaganda are base values

---

[16] The values for each individual are obviously different, but I will argue in later chapters that there are certain core values that are being manipulated.

already present in the socio-political framework which are being called upon to elicit action.

Stereotyping propaganda is used in an effort to reinforce existing values. From the leader's perspective, this includes both reinforcing the values and beliefs of individual or group A by comparing A to B, and at the same time, downplaying the values and beliefs of B. This form of propaganda strengthens or creates images which "satisf(y) man's need for release and certainty," as well as "ease his tensions and compensate for his frustrations."[17] It mirrors Aristotle's concept of epideictic rhetoric.[18]

Finally, there is visionary propaganda. A call is made by the leader to return to the values of the past or to hope for certain values in the future. A good example of recalling past ideals can be found in Robert N. Bellah's *Habits of the Heart*. In it, he suggests that Americans should either return to the republican values of the past or reinforce the "biblical strand" present in the United States. One of these options would apparently assist in eliminating the "radical individualism" already present in America.[19] Using propaganda to promote a better future can easily be seen in socialist or communist writings. Charles Fourier envisioned his idea of the ideal world embodied in the Phalanx where individuals would eliminate the drudgeries of both life and work through his concept of "passionate attraction."[20] Karl Marx's notion of the Communist state relies on propaganda

---

[17] Jaques Ellul, *Propaganda: The Formation of Men's Attitudes*, (New York: Alfred A. Knopf, 1965) 174.

[18] See Aristotle's Rhetoric, H.G. Apostle and L.P. Gearson, *Aristotle's Selected Works*, (Grinnel: The Peripatetic Press, 1991).

[19] Robert N. Bellah et. al, *Habits of the Heart*, (New York: Harper and Row Publishers, 1985).

[20] *See* Charles Fourier, *Utopian Socialism*, ed. Nancy Love, Dogmas and Dreams, (Chantham: Chantham House Publishers, Inc., 1991) 185-206.

which suggests that the future will be a world free of "exploitation of one part of society by another."[21]

Chapters five will answer the question: "What does propaganda hope to accomplish?" Using James MacGregor Burns' notion of the purposes of leadership, I will explain why propaganda is used in certain situations.[22] Chapter five will deal with the use of propaganda in "transactional" leadership. Burns suggests that governing is transactional "when one person takes the initiative in making contact with others for the purpose of an exchange of valued things."[23] This type of political relationship is posited in the interests of individuals. I will argue that Machiavellian politics is transactional, in that it functions under a "give and take" system but the goal is to take more than one gives.

The use of propaganda in transforming leadership will also be discussed. Burns defines it as leading in an attempt to "raise [both leader and followers] to higher levels of motivation and morality."[24] Governing in this manner has many moralistic overtones. As Burns suggests, "transforming leadership ultimately becomes moral in that it raises the level of human conduct and ethical aspiration of both leader and led, and thus it has a transforming effect on both."[25]

In effect, the primary purpose of this research paper is to explore the function and purpose of propaganda and the means by which the leader uses it. Stated in simpler terms: "What does it do?", "How does it do it?", and "Why is it

---

[21] Karl Marx, *The Communist Manifesto*, (New York: W.W. Norton and Co., 1988) 74.

[22] *See* James MacGregor Burns, *Leadership*, (London, Harper Torchbooks, 1978), *The Power to Lead*, (New York: Simon and Schuster, 1984) and an insightful interview of Burns in *Presidential Studies Quarterly*, vol. 16 no. 3, 1986, 528-542 for a look at his theory behind leadership.

[23] James MacGregor Burns, *Leadership*, (London, Harper Torchbooks, 1978) 19.

[24] Ibid, 20.

[25] Ibid, 20.

done?" The sixth chapter will build upon the preceding chapters in order to move a step further. The use of propaganda by the Presidents will now be placed in the context of the democratic system itself. Using Robert A. Dahl's notion of a polyarchal pluralist society, it will be explained why and how democracy serves the needs of the propagandist.[26]

Another goal of chapter six is to explore the effects of propaganda on democracy. Is propaganda a threat to democracy or does is it merely an outgrowth of its use? This section involves speculation on what could happen given the current trends in manipulation. These questions will be answered using theorists such as Harold D. Lasswell, Herbert Marcuse, and Jaques Ellul. Finally, a concluding chapter will summarize the findings of this research and presage the future use and effects of propaganda in our society.

---

[26] *See* Robert A. Dahl, *A Preface to Democratic Theory*, (Chicago: University of Chicago Press, 1956); *Modern Political Analysis*; *Dilemmas of Pluralist Democracy: Autonomy vs. Control*, (New Haven: Yale University Press, 1982); and *Polyarchy*, (New Haven: Yale University Press, 1971).

Chapter Two:

A Theoretical Basis for Propaganda

"Man is a political animal by nature; he is a scientist by chance or choice; he is a moralist because he is a man. Man is born to seek power, yet his actual condition makes him a slave to the power of others. Man is born a slave, but everywhere he wants to be a master."[27]

– Hans J. Morgenthau

Morgenthau in suggesting that "man is born a slave, but everywhere he wants to be a master" recognizes the basic concept of power in politics; that is, the individual belongs to a system where he is both leader and follower. All individuals maintain a certain degree of power, but in one manner or another, are controlled by the power of others.[28] This causes a pyramidal power structure (see Fig. 2.1).

---

[27] Hans J. Morgenthau, *Scientific Man vs. Power Politics*, (Chicago, The University of Chicago Press, 1946) 168.

[28] John Gaventa recognizes three dimensions of power: "(1) prevalence of A (through superior bargaining resources), (2) construction of barriers against participation of B, and (3) influencing or shaping of consciousness of B about inequalities." John Gaventa, *Power and Powerlessness*, (Urbana: The University of Illinois Press, 1980) 21.

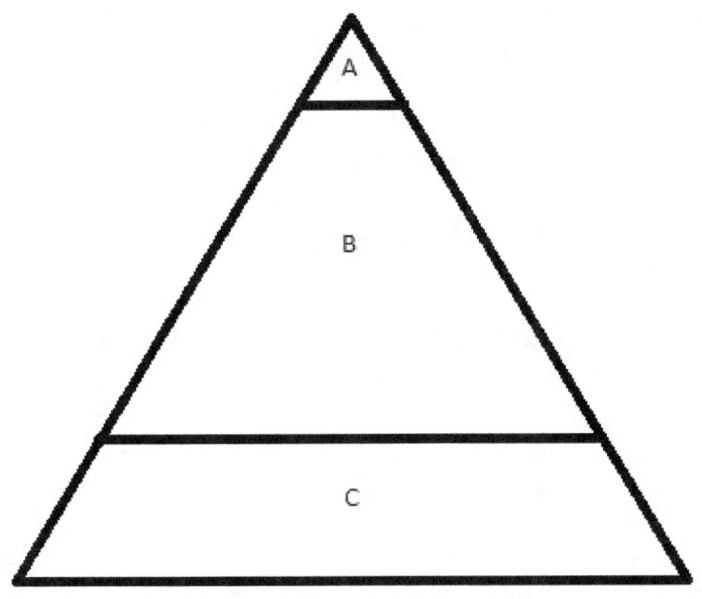
Pyramidal Power Structure - Fig. 2.1

In this system, power can be thought of as a tangible entity -- a good, governed by the laws of scarcity. There are varying degrees of power. The leader, for example, could be placed at point A near the apex of the pyramid; a middle income voter at point B and a homeless person at point C. No individual can reach the apex or base of the pyramid -- leaders are always constrained in one manner or another, whether it be by domestic voters or foreign dictators, whereas the homeless can exert even minimal amounts of power over their children or others at their level. Power or lack thereof is, therefore, not an absolute.

Upon entering the world, the *homo politicus*[29] is placed in an environment where each person seeks to obtain

---

[29] Although I recognize Robert A. Dahl's distinction between *homo civicus* and *politicus*, I will only discuss the political person and his actions in this context. See Robert A. Dahl, "The Concept of Power," in Roderick Bell, David M. Edwards, R. Harrison Wagner, eds., *Political Power: A Reader in Theory and*

and maintain the largest possible quantum of power. Given that power is a scarce good, a constant tension that is almost Hobbesian in nature exists in society. This tension results from a disparity in power and can take the form of anxiety, hostility, depression, and the like.

How does power create tension? Joseph R. Gusfield's notion of class/status politics adequately illustrates this concept.[30]

Joseph Gusfield's Class/Status Model
Fig. 2.2

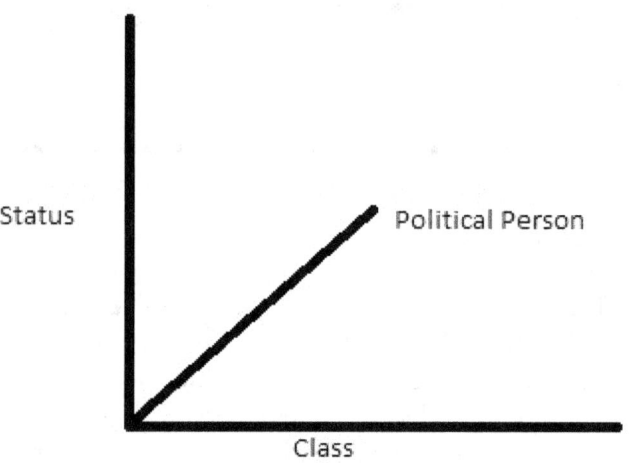

In this graph, a move upwards along the vertical axis indicates an increase in status or prestige. Horizontal movement towards the right indicates an augmentation of monetary worth. Motion in both directions suggests an overall increase in power as illustrated by the diagonal line in Figure 2.2. In this framework, in order to gain power, one

---

Research, (New York: Free Press, 1969), p. 80, reprinted from *Behavioral Science*, 2 (1957), 201-205.

[30] Joseph Gusfield, *Symbolic Crusade*, (Urbana: University of Illinois Press, 1963) 13-15. This model is used in relation to the American experience.

must obtain it from others. A power increase for one individual is counteracted by a decrease for another, thereby creating tension.

How then does one succeed in this system? The most successful player will recognize the tension which emerges from power and compensate for it. If he can make others believe that his increased influence or political strength is for the common good or serves a specific purpose, then any animosity caused by a loss in the power of others would be moderated.

Three political theorists recognize the importance of assuaging tension and base many of their theories around this knowledge. Niccolò Machiavelli speaks of avoiding hatred in dealing with the masses. This hatred can be caused by the usurpation or misuse of power by the leader. Machiavelli advocates the use of deceptive tactics to disguise the true motives of the leader or prince. This would compensate for the tension created. Harold D. Lasswell acknowledges the tension and anxiety present within the personality as well as the tension created through international conflict. He also sees the role of the propagandist as exploiter of this tension. Finally, Jaques Ellul sees propaganda by glossing over reality with a ready-made image as decreasing the tension caused by the power disparity. In the following pages, the ideas of each theorist will be discussed for two reasons: (1) to illustrate the importance of tension in society which I will later discuss in chapter 3 and (2) to provide a theoretical basis for the following chapters dealing with propaganda, leadership, and democracy. Each of the philosophers has provided not only a framework for this study but has also guided my approach to the subject.

Niccolò Machiavelli

Throughout his works, Niccolò Machiavelli recognizes the supreme importance of power in politics. It moves armies, creates nations, destroys life, and spares it. He explores the weapons of personal gain and demonstrates how one can wield them. These methods, posited in his nihilistic views, often include immoral tactics which have subsequently labeled him, "the man whose name has become synonymous with evil."[31] In order to fully comprehend "the most objectionable political and moral controversies...of our time,"[32] necessitates an in-depth examination of Machiavelli's concept of human nature. From this starting point, one can further venture into the political spectrum and understand how a person interacts as an automaton within it.

First and foremost, any endeavor to define Machiavelli's theories must begin with a discussion of his views on human nature in general. His rationale for an individual's actions does not appear as a clear-cut and orderly argument but as a piecemeal collection of thoughts found throughout his works. Unlike most philosophers, he finds humans to be inherently evil -- "all men are evil in that they will always express the wickedness of their spirit whenever they have the opportunity."[33]

How, then, does one explain righteousness or good deeds? Machiavelli addresses this point by saying that the individual is only moral out of Necessità or necessity, otherwise an individual will act in his/her own self-interest. Machiavelli sees Necessità as almost a divine force, in that

---

[31] Niccolò Machiavelli, *The Prince*, trans. Christian E. Detmold, ed. Lester G. Crocker (New York: Washington Square Press, Inc., 1968) 1.

[32] Count Carlo Sforza, *The Living Thoughts of Machiavelli*, (New York: Fawcett Publications, 1959) 11.

[33] Niccolò Machiavelli, *The Portable Machiavelli*, (New York: Penguin Books, 1979) 182.

it is inspirational but acts on an individual as an outside impetus as does Fortuna. It is not unyielding like the Greek concept of fate, but merely acts as a guide in an individual's life. According to Felix Gilbert, "In whatever situation man finds himself the final outcome depends on his response to the conditions which Necessità has produced."[34]

If persons do not act at the opportune time, they suffer the consequences of their passivity and are forced to act in a desperate manner. As Machiavelli states, one should "pretend to do out of generosity what must be done out of necessity;" because, "prudent men make a virtue out of necessity,"[35] This illusion of generosity not only allows the ruler or regime to act in a demanding time, but also creates favorable public opinion. Machiavelli, then, sees all good deeds resulting from self-interested acts based on demanding or the appearance of demanding circumstances.

If an individual does act in self-interest what is his/her primary goal? Machiavelli mentions several desires in men throughout The Prince and The Discourses such as glory or power; but his/her theories posit a general view of an individual's central longing for the promotion of his/her own personal gain regardless of the form it assumes. Even property and possessions are just another manifestation of the want for personal gain. This is apparently a universal concept for Machiavelli -- "in all cities and all peoples there still exist, and have always existed, the same desires and passions."[36]

In *The Prince*, Machiavelli establishes a guide for rulers or would-be rulers on the roles of manipulation, the pitfalls of leadership, and the means to ascendancy. All of this was done with the knowledge that individual's desire is to better his/her current conditions or standing in life. To

---

[34] Felix Gilbert, "Fortune, Necessity, and Virtue," *The Prince*, (New York: W.W. Norton and Co., 1992) 150-155.

[35] *The Portable Machiavelli*, 273.

[36] Ibid, 252.

obtain this end, Machiavelli suggests that one "should not depart from the good if he can hold to it, but he should be ready to enter in evil if he has to."[37] An individual should, therefore, do whatever possible to insure his/her success. Standards, laws, and morals do not guide men; rather, they are impediments or obstacles to the individual's objectives. The most successful leaders, those who are able to stay in power the longest, rise above these constraints in one way or another.

Given that an individual's desire is to achieve goals what are the means available to accomplish same? According to Machiavelli, there are four routes to ascendancy: virtù, Fortuna or luck, crime, or "the rise of a private citizen to supreme authority in his land through the choice of his fellow citizens,"[38] (see fig. 2.3).

The Machiavellian Pyramid Viewed from Above

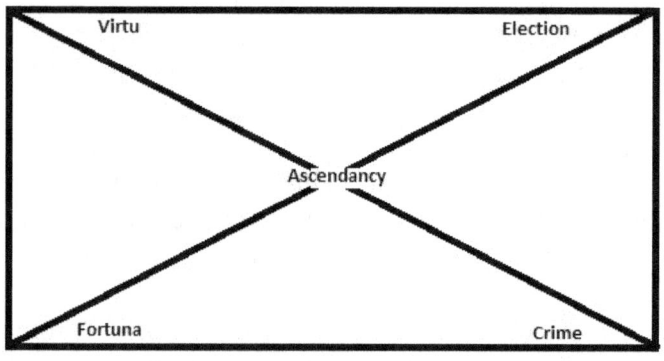

Fig. 2.3

---

[37] Niccolò Machiavelli, *The Prince* (New York: Washington Square Press, 1968) 77-79.

[38] *The Portable Machiavelli*, 261.

The first means of ascendancy involves the use of one's own talents. Machiavelli "concentrated all his real and supreme values in what he called virtù."[39] Virtù is not easily translated and has been used synonymously with talent, ability, strength, courage, and so on. Many intellectuals have sought to categorize virtù in various forms such as civic and heroic.[40] J.H. Whitfield, on the contrary, fails to see any notion of virtù in Machiavelli's works.[41] The uses of virtù by Machiavelli can be summarized by defining it as follows: all talents or virtues which can lead an individual or a republic to their desired goal.

What, then, are the qualities found in virtù which are necessary for leadership? In chapters XV-XXIII of The Prince, Machiavelli lists several attributes which would aid in controlling power, such as being parsimonious rather than generous and cruel rather than clement. Determination and hard work are highly regarded. He argues that one "must never idle away his days of peace but vigorously make capital that will pay off in times of adversity."[42] A ruler must also imitate the actions of both the lion and the fox. The individual must be strong and be prepared to abandon the laws and use force if necessary.[43] He must also be cunning like a fox through deception and manipulation.[44]

Machiavelli, however, places more faith in fraud and deception than in force alone. In The Discourses, he states,

---

[39] F. Meinecke, *Machiavellism: The Doctrine of Raison d'Etat and Its Place in Modern History*, tr. Douglas Scott (London and New Haven, 1957) 31.

[40] John Plamenatz discusses his ideas of different categories of virtù in "In Search of Machiavellian Virtù," *The Political Calculus*, (Toronto: University of Toronto, 1972) 157-178.

[41] J.H. Whitfield, *Machiavelli*, (Blackwell, 1947) 95.

[42] *The Prince*, (New York: W. W. Norton and Co., 1992) 17.

[43] Ibid, 48.

[44] Many American Presidents have fit this model. Franklin D. Roosevelt exhibited the perfect mixture of both power and cunning. *See* James MacGregor Burns, *Roosevelt: The Lion and the Fox*, (New York: Harcourt Brace Jovanovich, 1956).

"I believe it to be very true that rarely or never do men of humble station rise to high ranks without force and without fraud," but "nor do I believe that force by itself will ever suffice, although fraud alone can surely suffice."[45] Given this, the leader must be more fox than lion. Machiavelli's concept of deception involves the use of manipulation in order to act in one's own self-interest. In The Prince, he states that the greatest rulers are those who are able to pretend to possess all of the desired characteristics of a prince; for, "a wise prince will think of ways to keep his citizens of every sort and under every circumstance dependent on the state and on him."[46] To create this appearance a ruler should appear to be "merciful, truthful, humane, sincere, and religious."[47] But in order to maintain a hold on power, the individual must be prepared to act in a contrary manner. Machiavelli argues that the populace readily accepts showmanship and rhetoric over true merit or political strength because "they are deceived by a false appearance of good unless they are persuaded otherwise."[48] The statements in Chapter XVIII of The Prince summarize his ideas-- "Men are so simple of mind, and so much dominated by their immediate needs, that a deceitful man will always find plenty who are ready to be deceived."[49]

When using the tactics of force and deception, Machiavelli reiterates one commandment, that it is better to be feared than loved, but an individual must avoid being hated by the people. Both love and fear move people to action but love is not as binding of an emotion as fear. "Love is a link of obligation which men, because they are rotten, will break any time they think doing so serves their

[45] Niccolò Machiavelli, *The Portable Machiavelli*, (New York: Penguin Books, 1979) 314, italics added for emphasis.

[46] *The Prince*, (New York: W. W. Norton and Co., 1992) 30.

[47] Ibid, 48.

[48] *The Portable Machiavelli*, 274.

[49] *The Prince*, 48.

advantage."[50] Fear, on the other hand, causes men to act out of intimidation and the fear of punishment which might accompany failure.

Machiavelli also suggests that leaders should look to the past as a guide to the present. His non-progressive view of history allows for predictable results through careful observation of the accomplishments of rulers. In The Prince, he urges the use of prudence -- one "should always follow the footsteps of the great and imitate those who have been supreme."[51] He looks to the Romans and uses them as examples in many cases. As he states in The Art of War: "And if we consider the practice and institutions observed by the old Romans, we shall find many things worthy of imitation."[52] For Machiavelli, history repeats itself continually, therefore, "reason or prudence will decide the prince's conduct on the basis of his immediate or proximate goals."[53] There are no notions of progress toward democracy as suggested by Harold D. Lasswell or the debilitation of an individual as with Rousseau, but merely a continuous timeline where one can examine the deeds of leaders at any point.[54]

The theories of Niccolò Machiavelli are clearly the cornerstone of modern day politics. With tools such as propaganda available, the wise politician need only to appear to be the ideal citizen. Reality and truth have faded and have become yet another weapon used by the ingenious ruler. Politics has, therefore, become Machiavellian in nature -- the leader must be above morality, above religion, and even

---

[50] Ibid, 46.

[51] The Prince, (New York: W.W. Norton and Co., 1992) 15.

[52] Niccolò Machiavelli, *The Art of War*, (New York: A Da Capo Press, 1990) 12.

[53] Sebastian de Grazia, *Machiavelli in Hell*, (New York, Vintage Books, 1989) 310.

[54] *The Prince* presents itself not only as a guide to prudence but also as a prudential work in and of itself. *See* Eugene Garver, *Machiavelli and the History of Prudence*, (Madison: University of Wisconsin Press, 1987).

above politics. Harold D. Lasswell builds upon the teachings of Niccolò Machiavelli by delving into the personality structure of leaders and examining the function and use of propaganda in the modern political context.

Harold D. Lasswell

Arguably one of the greatest theorists of our time, Harold D. Lasswell dedicated his life to three main ideas -- "description, prediction, and control."[55] As a political scientist, Lasswell was naturally interested in the role of the leader, and how he or she was able to effectively control the minds of others especially through the use of propaganda. In order to fully understand the intricacies of Lasswell's work on propaganda, his ideas dealing with the "description" of the political person must be explored.

Lasswell in creating his notion of political psychology borrowed directly from the works of Sigmund Freud. For example, he maintains that there is a "triple-appeal principle" to personality involving the id, ego, and superego.[56] In *World Politics and Personal Insecurity*, he identifies and explains the tensions that result from the interaction of these three forces. Hostility and tension are created by the conflicting mores, counter-mores, and expediencies. Instead of turning this tension inwards in the form of self-degradation or depression, "anxieties ...may be effectively abolished by displacing hostilities upon wives, secretaries, or chauffeurs; or by orgiastic and diffuse release

[55] Robert Horowitz, "Scientific Propaganda," in *Essays on the Scientific Study of Politics*, (New York: Holt, Rinehart, and Winston, Inc., 1962) 227.

[56] Harold D. Lasswell, "The Triple-Appeal Principle: A Contribution of Psychoanalysis to Political and Social Science." *American Journal of Sociology*, 37 (1932): 523-538.

in... alcoholism" and the like.[57] In suggesting that hostility is a function of displaced tension, Lasswell implies that the antagonistic forces of our personality are a major cause of international conflict.

In an earlier work, Psychopathology and Politics, Lasswell further develops the notion of the political personality. Based upon the works of Eduard Spranger, he formulates the following equation: $p\} d\} r = P$ "where p equals private motives; d equals displacement onto a public object; r equals rationalization in terms of public interest; P equals the political person; and } equals transformed into."[58] In other words, the individual displaces his/her feelings (usually anxiety based) onto a public object, and then justifies it through political interests.

Lasswell recognizes three primary political character types based on this formula -- the agitator, administrator, and theorist. The agitator is a person of action; one who stirs up trouble. Most important to the agitator is the "emotional response of the public."[59] The need for attention and narcissistic tendencies cause him/her to seek public acceptance rationalized through the guise of politics. Administrators are "distinguished by the value which they place upon the coordination of effort in continuing activity."[60] Displacing their obsessive-compulsive behavior, administrators seek management to create stability and control in their lives. They have difficulty in defining the ego and suppress tension as a result. Lasswell later termed this type "the bureaucrat."[61] The final type, the theorist or

---

57 Harold D. Lasswell, *World Politics and Personal Insecurity*, (New York: Whittlesey House, 1935) 69.

58 Harold D. Lasswell, *Psychopathology and Politics*, (Chicago: University of Chicago Press, 1930) 75-76.

59 Ibid, 78.

60 Ibid, 263.

61 Harold D. Lasswell, *Power and Personality*, (New York: W.W. Norton and Co., 1948) 89.

detached character, is somewhat compulsive but lacks the intensity of the agitator or administrator. Lasswell suggests that he is devoid of "lively emotional states."[62]

"To what extent are we in ignorance of our own motives and accustomed to improvise merely plausible explanations of and to ourselves?"[63] In attempting to answer this question, Harold Lasswell implies that politics is merely a formulation of character flaws. The *homo politicus* is blinded by inner desires and urges and cannot see beyond his its own rationalizations: "Political acts depend upon the symbolization of the discontent of the individual in terms of a more inclusive self which champions a set of demands for social action."[64] Politics, therefore, is only an outlet for tension within the personality.

What are the core values which political person seeks? According to Harold Lasswell in *Politics: Who Gets What, When, How*, they are "deference, income, and safety."[65] In subsequent works such as *The Political Writings and Power and Personality*, he expands these values but still uses income, safety, and deference as the main categories.[66] The political person seeks to maximize and consolidate

---

[62] Ibid, 93. Although Lasswell has clearly defined several of the major political types, he has not characterized every possibility. For example, the Machiavellian would be fully aware of his own desires and would consciously use rationalizations to manipulate others -- p} r = P instead of p } d } r = P. His motives would not be displaced on public objects but merely disguised through politics.

[63] *Psychopathology and Politics*, 20.

[64] Ibid, 265.

[65] Harold D. Lasswell, *Politics: Who Gets What, When, and How*, (Cleveland: Meridian Books, 1958) 13. Income, safety, and deference come from Thomas Hobbes' quote in *Leviathan*: "that in the nature of man, we find three principal causes of quarrel. First, competition; second, diffidence, thirdly, glory. The first maketh man invade for gain; the second for safety; and the third, for reputation." Thomas Hobbes, *Leviathan*, (New York: Penguin Books, 1968) 185.

[66] For example, in the *The Political Writings*, he states, "safety can be treated as equivalent to well-being, income to wealth, and deference, if desired, to the sub-divided list comprising power, respect, affection, rectitude." Harold D. Lasswell, *The Political Writings*, (Illinois: Glencoe, 1951) 475, n. 20.

his/her hold on each. Lasswell called this the "maximization postulate" and based it on his ideas of the I-D (Indulgence-Deprivation) ratio:

> Indulgence is increase in influence; deprivation is decrease...It follows from the definitions that all demands are to maximize indulgence over deprivation for the identified self, and that behavior is based on expectations as to the I-D ratio.[67]

Because safety, deference, and income are scarce items, Lasswell views society much like Hobbes' state of war. Men, therefore, face not only the tension and hostility created internally by their own personalities, but also from the external threats to their core values.

As Robert Horowitz suggests, "The struggle for safety, income, and deference is, in its most general statement, the struggle for power."[68] Those who control the values have the power or are the "who" in the "who gets what, when, how." The quest for power causes increased entropy in society. For this reason, Lasswell argues that politics must be used for prevention. Power should be diffuse and limited -- "the idea of preventative politics...draws attention squarely to the central problem of reducing the level of strain and maladaptation in society."[69]

How, then, can politics be used for prevention? Lasswell answered this question through his concepts of propaganda.[70] In Propaganda Technique in the World War,

---

[67] Harold D. Lasswell and Abraham Kaplan, *Power and Society: A Framework for Political Inquiry*, (New Haven: Yale University Press, 1950) 61-62.

[68] *Essays on the Scientific Study of Politics*, 263.

[69] *Psychopathology and Politics*, 197.

[70] See Harold D. Lasswell's *Propaganda Technique in the World War; Propaganda, Communication, and Public Opinion; Propaganda in War and Crisis: Materials for American Policy*; and *Propaganda and World Public Order: The Legal Regulation of the Ideological Instrument of Coercion*. Harold

he states, "propaganda is concerned with the management of opinions and attitudes by the direct manipulation of social suggestion rather than by altering other conditions in the environment or in the organism."[71] He goes on to say that propaganda involves "skillfully guiding the minds of men."[72] In using propaganda, Lasswell states that it must be "catholic in its appeal."[73] It must touch every individual and involve "the repetition of ideas."[74] Propaganda is only effective when it is able to identify with the people.[75] Prejudices should be invoked and taken advantage of when possible. As Lasswell suggests:

> Successful propaganda depends upon the adroit use of means under favourable conditions...A propagandist can alter the organization of his activities, modify the streams of suggestion which he releases, and substitute one device of communication for another, but he must adjust himself to traditional prejudices, to certain objective facts of international life, and to the general tension level of the community.[76]

D. Lasswell, *Propaganda Technique in the World War*, (New York: Adolf A. Knopf, 1927) 9.

[71] Harold D. Lasswell, *Propaganda Technique in the World War,* (New York: Adolf A. Knopf, 1927) 9.

[72] Harold D. Lasswell, "The Garrison State and Specialists on Violence," *The Analysis of Political Behaviour*, p. 149.

[73] *Propaganda Technique in the World War*, 201.

[74] Ibid, 11.

[75] This process of identification involves the use of symbols. In *World Politics and Personal Insecurity*, Lasswell states that the propagandist should concentrate on "controlling mass insecurity by manipulating significant symbols." (25) He goes on to say that, "identification with any particular symbol by any person at any phase of his career line initiates a complex process of symbol elaboration" where the individual "reads into this symbol the loves and hopes of his entire personality." (39). Murray Edelman also argues that symbols provide "an encompassing principle that will introduce stability and predictability into this explosive clash of interests." Murray Edelman, *The Symbolic Uses of Politics*, (Urbana: The University of Illinois Press, 1964) 19.

[76] *Propaganda Technique in the World War,* 185.

In other words, the role of the propagandist involves paying close attention to the existing political climate and exploiting the tension level in society. Propaganda can easily incite people to action when tension levels are high. What exactly is this tension level? It is the cumulative amount of stress in a society which can include "public anxiety, nervousness, irritability, unrest, discontent or strain."[77] This tension level is the cornerstone of propaganda. In a war time situation, the tension level is very high, and "the propagandist who deals with a community when its tension level is high, finds that a reservoir of explosive energy can be touched off by the same small match which would normally ignite a bonfire."[78] In other words, propaganda provides the activating energy necessary to initiate change. If, however, anxiety is not at a level where the minds of men can be easily manipulated, it is the role of the propagandist to create tension slowly and methodically.

After studying and recognizing the importance of propaganda in wars, Lasswell carried his studies further into the realm of democratic propaganda. He believed in preventative politics or limiting the consolidation of power.[79] Propaganda would help achieve this goal. Although democracy rested in the hands of the masses, Lasswell saw the general public as incapable of supporting his notions of positive liberalism. He questioned whether they were "the best judges of their own interest."[80] It was,

---

[77] Ibid, 190.

[78] Ibid, 190.

[79] Here, Lasswell provides a contrast with Machiavelli's ideas of the self-interested search for power.

[80] Harold D. Lasswell, "Propaganda," *Encyclopedia of the Social Sciences*, (New York: The Macmillan Company, 1934), vol. XII, p. 527. George J. Graham, Jr. makes an interesting point: "Although Lasswell at times talked as if an intellectual elite might arise, the important point is that the policy sciences generate and respond to knowledge needs for better social development." George J. Graham, Jr., "'The Policy Orientation' and the Theoretical

therefore, up to the propagandist to instruct the masses and "create symbols which are not only popular but which bring about positive realignments of behavior."[81] It would be the job of the propagandist to lead the public away from the ideas of totalitarianism and the garrison state towards Lasswell's idea of the free-man commonwealth.

Re-instilling the democratic character was essential for the "utter annihilation of that sphere of life and discourse characterized by power."[82] In The Political Writings, Lasswell discusses the democratic character extensively. It involves "the maintenance of an open as against a closed ego," and is "disposed to share rather than to hoard or to monopolize."[83] "Human dignity" is also respected and "realized in theory and fact."[84] Basically, Lasswell's notion of democracy involves the compassion of Rousseau achieved through a Hobbesian state with a leader using Machiavelli's tactics. Robert Horowitz notes that Lasswell has mistakenly fallen in the trap of his own work. His theories are no different than those of Karl Marx whom he constantly criticizes:

> While inviting the assistance of like-minded academics who long to pull "the strings of Punch and Judy," the aspiring puppet master cavorts upon a stage built by others. The Master Propagandist is himself the victim of Propaganda.[85]

Development of Political Science," *Handbook of Political Theory and Political Science*, (New York: Greenwood Press, 1988) 159.

[81] Ibid, 527.

[82] *Essays on the Scientific Study of Politics*, 292.

[83] *The Political Writings*, 495, 498 respectively.

[84] Ibid, 473.

[85] *Essays on the Scientific Study of Politics*, 304. I disagree with Horowitz's conclusion. Lasswell was not a "tool of certain modern political philosophers," (303). It is clear that he was influenced by the works of others such as Spranger and Lippman but his theories are unique. No other theorist before his time applied Freudian teachings to politics with such vigor. Lasswell clearly fell into

Harold Lasswell clearly laid the ground work for future studies of propaganda and psychopathology in politics. His work was and will be the theoretical guidepost for years to come.

Jaques Ellul

Although his primary concentration has dealt with Christianity and religious topics, Jaques Ellul has greatly contributed to the study of propaganda. In *Propaganda: The Formation of Men's Attitudes*, he discusses the so-called "new propaganda." This form of manipulation not only includes the negative connotations associated with propaganda, i.e. its use in wars, but also recognizes its use in the modern political environment -- "the aim of modern propaganda is no longer to modify ideas, but to provoke action."[86]   It permeates every aspect of society, and according to Ellul is essential for the continuation of the technological society.

---

the trap of using propaganda with an elitist attitude, but I suggest that this was done for more than just egotistical reasons. In *World Politics and Personal Insecurity*, one of his earlier works, he clearly outlines what is needed for an "American *Capital*." or a propagandistic work similar to *Das Capital*. He lists nine requirements most of which are too vague to make any connections but some of them show remarkable similarities to Lasswell's idea of the "psychoanalytocracy." For example, his books are "systematic and quantitative" -- his use of the configurative analysis, developmental construct, and equilibrium analysis. "The key words and the style must be invidious" -- garrison state and his attacks on Marx "The prescription should be activistic" -- Lasswell continually calls for other social scientists to join his cause and rise up to instruct the world (219). Although I am sure he believed his theories wholeheartedly, his presentation of them might have been influenced by this early analysis of propagandistic work.

[86] Jaques Ellul, *Propaganda: The Formation of Men's Attitudes,* (New York: Alfred A. Knopf, 1965) 25.

What are the guidelines for using modern propaganda? Ellul argues that it must "address itself at one and the same time to the individual and to the masses."[87] Second, it must be pervasive in its approach -- all institutions and aspects of society should reflect propagandistic rhetoric. Third, it "must be continuous and lasting -- continuous in that it must not leave any gaps, but must fill the citizen's whole day and all his days; lasting in that it must function over a very long period of time."[88] Fourth, the use of propaganda must be done at the right moment -- "man can be captured and mobilized only if there is consonance between his own deep social beliefs and those underlying the propaganda directed at him."[89]

Fifth, the propagandist builds upon a previously established framework of sociological and ideological values; "he must know the sentiments and opinions, the current tendencies and the stereotypes among the public he is trying to reach."[90] Prejudices and other pre-existing notions among the populace are used frequently. The manipulator will act and speak using inconsistencies and vague pleas or appeals but will "never make a direct attack on an established, reasoned, durable opinion."[91] In other words, propaganda will always be based on ideas already present in the community.

How does propaganda affect those influenced by it? Propaganda can be thought of as an addictive drug. It fulfills certain desires and needs and in order to satisfy these wants, greater quantities of it must be used as time goes by. Like Lasswell, Ellul recognizes the anxiety and tension present in society. The political person searches for stability and continuity in life. Propaganda provides this. It acts as a

---

[87] Ibid, 6.

[88] Ibid, 17.

[89] Ibid, 43.

[90] Ibid, 34.

[91] Ibid, 34.

blanket covering any incongruities in society while providing an ever-ready explanation or course of action for the individual to follow. It gives him "certainty."[92]

Propaganda also bolsters self-esteem and feelings of self-worth. The individual obtains a sense of belonging and it allows "him to assert himself" while satisfying "his need for active participation."[93] Most importantly, propaganda provides justification. It answers the bigger questions in life "What is my purpose here?", "What do I believe in?", etc. It guides the person and convinces him/her that "he (she) is on the right path."[94]

Ellul divides propaganda into various useful categories. He distinguishes between political and sociological propaganda. Political propaganda "involves techniques of influence employed by a government...with a view to changing the behavior of the public."[95] This includes manipulative attempts by other political institutions as well. The second form entails the use of integrating and unifying tactics. Ideologies are a type of sociological propaganda. Ellul defines it as:

> the group of manifestations by which any society seeks to integrate the maximum number of individuals into itself, to unify its members' behavior according to a pattern, to spread its style of life abroad, and thus to impose itself on other groups.

Propaganda can, therefore, be two fold. It can first attack or buttress beliefs through political propaganda and then seek

---

[92] Ibid, 184.

[93] Ibid, 185

[94] Ibid, 185.

[95] Ibid, 62.

to reaffirm or negate the larger context of sociological propaganda (see fig. 2.4).[96]

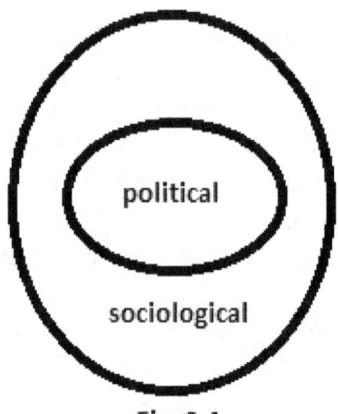

political

sociological

Fig. 2.4

Ellul also distinguishes between vertical and horizontal propaganda. Vertical propaganda is similar to James MacGregor Burns' notion of transactional leadership. Both involve a leader-follower relationship. It is basically a manipulative attempt by a leader or superior to incite action. Horizontal propaganda, on the other hand, "is made inside the group (not from the top), where, in principle, all individuals are equal and there is no leader."[97] Ellul gives the example of Chinese propaganda where careful attention is given to the thoughts of each member of a group before coming to a decision.

Unlike Harold Lasswell, Ellul sees propaganda as an evil. It "violates the masses and insidiously determines the citizen's behavior -- it exercises repressive coercion, but on

---

[96] Political and sociological propagandas are very similar to the propaganda of agitation and integration that Ellul discusses later.

[97] Ibid, 81.

a larger scale."[98]   Propaganda undermines rationality, autonomy, and, at a basic level, human dignity. Through propaganda, a universe is created "in which everything is translated into images, in which everything is image."[99] Because of the use of propaganda, a condition in society forms where urgency is inter-twined with the superfluous. Propaganda confuses the facts and truth and gives politics in general an "illusory face."[100]Not only is propaganda destructive to democracy, but it also supports the existing oppression under the technological society.

What is the technological society? According to Ellul, the importance placed on efficiency has created the modern world -- a world without compassion. The political person is tricked into believing that technology or technique as he calls it, is a good thing while he stands in the unemployment line. Ellul take a Marxian stance towards capitalism. He suggests "technological progress is a function of bourgeois money."[101] Modernity has caused a general demoralization of mankind. In the words of Christopher Lasch, society has become analogous to the prostitute who:

> best exemplifies the qualities indispensable to success in American society...She is a loner, dependent on others only as a hawk depends on chickens...even the most intimate encounters become a form of mutual exploitation. [102]

---

[98] Jaques Ellul, *The Political Illusion*, (New York: Vintage Books, 1967) 77.

[99] Ibid, 113. Also see Daniel J. Boorstin, The Image, (New York: Vintage Books, 1987) and Jean Baudrillard, The Illusion of the End, (Oxford: Polity Press, 1994).

[100] Ibid, 67. "The people will fancy an appearance of freedom; illusion will be their native land." -- Saint-Just.

[101] Jaques Ellul, The Technological Society, (New York: Vintage Books, 1964) 54.

[102] Christopher Lasch, *The Culture of Narcissism*, (New York: Warner Books, 1979) 125.

With the shift to gesellschaft, technology creates instruments which support its own existence. TV and the mass media created within the last five decades bombards the American public with news and information and according to Ginsberg and Shefter has become a main political player.[103] As Ellul argues in *The Technological System*, "technologies now make it possible to shape desire, and public opinion forms on that basis."[104]

The work of these theorists was instrumental in the construction of my ideas on propaganda and its use by leaders. I will continue discussing the work of Niccolò Machiavelli, Harold D. Lasswell, and Jaques Ellul by studying the subject of propaganda, and in particular, its relationship to leadership and democracy. In the ensuing chapters, I will allude to the theories of these men in order to answer the following questions: "How does propaganda function?", "In what manner is it used", and "What does it hope to accomplish?" In the next chapter, I will answer the first of these questions.

---

[103] Benjamin Ginsberg and Martin Shefter, *Politics by Other Means*, (New York: Basic Books, 1990).

[104] Jaques Ellul, *The Technological System*, (New York: Continuum, 1980) 37. See also Jaques Ellul, *The Technological Bluff*, (Grand Rapids: William B. Eerdmans Publishing Co., 1990) 54.

Chapter Three:

The Function of Propaganda

This chapter will explore the function of propaganda by answering the question: "What does it hope to accomplish?" Using examples from the modern day Presidency, I will explore the factors which are used by the propagandist to obtain a given result. I will also show that propaganda can be either positive, negative, or satisficing in its attempts to manipulate the anxiety and tension level (A-T level) in personalities.

Propaganda is a means to an end. It is the systematic and methodical attempt to sway the minds of others. In using it as a form of persuasion, the leader purposely attempts to reach his desired goals through social control. But how is this accomplished? How is the human mind so easily clouded by rhetoric and showmanship? The answers lie in personality structure.

The personality can be thought of as a complex matrix of components which simultaneously work dependently and independently to make decisions and format behavior. According to Sigmund Freud, the three primary components are the ego or self, the id or subconscious urges and desires, and the super-ego responsible for "moral restraint."[105] The ego can be considered a person's conscious thought. It is continually influenced by both the id and super-ego. This influence often causes the A-T level to rise. The super-ego creates feelings of guilt over the urges of the id which in turn fosters

---

[105] Sigmund Freud, *The Ego and the Id*, (New York: W.W. Norton and Co., 1960) 27.

a "feeling of uneasiness, a kind of anxiety."[106] This causes "other feelings of unpleasureable character (mental tension, sorrow, grief)."[107]

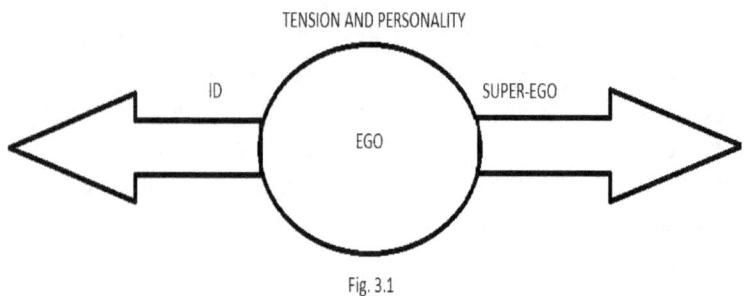

TENSION AND PERSONALITY

Fig. 3.1

As figure 3.1 illustrates, the ego is subjected to the influence of both the id and the super-ego. To maintain stability in the personality with a relatively stable A-T level, the two components must offset each other. If, however, the id or super-ego pulls the ego too far in one direction or the other, an imbalance is created.[108]

Tension and anxiety are not inherent in the political person but are learned over time. Mark R. Leary in Understanding Social Anxiety argues that anxiety and tension are learned through classical conditioning:

---

[106] Sigmund Freud, *Civilization and Its Discontents*, (W.W. Norton and Co., 1961) 99.

[107] Sigmund Freud, *The Problem of Anxiety*, (New York: W.W. Norton and Co., 1936) 91.

[108] Freud also discusses two other forces which create tension -- Eros and Thanatos. Eros is "the all-sustaining...narcissistic libido of the ego" or the "life-instinct." It seeks to build up and create. Thanatos, on the other hand, is the "death instinct" or the part of a person which seeks to destroy and diminish. See: Sigmund Freud, *Beyond the Pleasure Principle*, (London: The International Psycho-Analytical Press, 1922) 67.

Most psychologists maintain that human beings have few, if any inborn fears or anxieties. It is true that young babies show a "startle response" to certain stimuli such as loud noises and loss of physical support (i.e., falling), but babies do not naturally fear the wide variety of objects and events that evoke anxiety in older children and adults. According to the classical conditioning model, these fears develop when a neutral stimulus that is initially incapable of causing anxiety becomes paired or associated with stimuli that are capable of eliciting fear or anxiety. As a consequence of the stimuli being paired together over time, the initially neutral stimulus acquires the ability to elicit anxiety on its own.[109]

Tension and anxiety or lack thereof triggers the emergence of emotions. An increase in the A-T level can cause negative emotions such as fear, anger, distress, contempt, shame, and disgust.[110] A decrease can elicit any one or combination of the following positive emotions: joy, love, hope, acceptance, or pride.[111] It is this anxiety and tension level, which will now be referred to as the A-T level, that the propagandist manipulates.[112]

---

[109] Mark R. Leary, *Understanding Social Anxiety*, (Beverly Hills: Sage Publications, 1983) 31-32.

[110] Based on Silvan Tomkins list of primary emotions. See *Psychology: Themes and Variations*, 367. Harold Lasswell in *Propaganda Technique in the World War* has this to say about the tension level: "By the tension level is meant that condition of adaption or mal-adaption, which is variously described as public anxiety, nervousness, irritability, unrest, discontent or strain." (190).

[111] Ibid, 367.

[112] The Institute for Propaganda Analysis also suggests that emotion is the factor being manipulated by the propagandist:

"Observe that in all these devices our emotion is the stuff with which propagandists work. Without it they are helpless; with it, harnessing it to their purposes, they can make us zealots in behalf of the program they espouse. Propaganda as generally understood is expression of opinion or action by

In order to produce a desired outcome or to incite action, the propagandist can use three different types of propaganda, all of which affect the A-T level within the personality. *Positive* seeks to decrease, negative to increase, and satisficing to maintain the A-T level.[113] Murray Edelman observed the political effects of tension cause "great suspicion of critics of the status quo;"[114]thereby, influencing politics. Harold Lasswell underscores this idea in Psychopathology in Politics. He states, "the dynamic of politics is to be found in the tension level of the individuals in society."[115] In the following paragraphs, I will (1) define the different forms, (2) show how they influence the A-T level, and (3) use examples from the modern Presidency as evidence to support my claims.

When discussing the various forms of propaganda, the examples used will be somewhat constrained given the scope of the work. First, only the American system of government will be used. This allows the readers to not only

---

individuals or groups with reference to predetermined ends. Without the appeal to our emotion -- to our fears and to our courage, to our selfishness and unselfishness, to our loves and to our hates -- propagandists would influence few opinions and few actions." Institute for Propaganda Analysis, "How to Detect Propaganda," *Propaganda*, (New York: New York University Press, 1995) 222.

I have chosen the anxiety and tension within the personality as the manipulated factor, but I do recognize the role of emotion in creating or dissipating this anxiety and tension.

[113] In designing this classification, I used the basic terms positive and negative which are clearly not original terms. Isaiah Berlin refers to positive and negative forms of freedom in *Four Essays on Liberty*, Charles S. Hyneman in *The Supreme Court on Trial* to positive and negative forms of power, and even Jaques Ellul to positive and negative forms of propaganda which will be discussed later. See Isaiah Berlin, *Four Essays on Liberty*, (London: Oxford University Press, 1969) 122-134; Charles S. Hyneman, *The Supreme Court on Trial*, (New York: Atherton Press, 1963); Jaques Ellul, *Propaganda: The Formation of Men's Attitudes*, (New York: Alfred A. Knopf, 1965).

[114] Murray Edelman, *The Symbolic Uses of Politics*, (Urbana: University of Illinois Press, 1964) 177.

[115] *Psychopathology and Politics*, 185.

examine and compare the examples chosen based on their familiarity with the system, but to also confine the usage of propaganda to one particular regime. Each government obviously uses propaganda in a different fashion; for example, the Communist rhetoric of Cuba differs vastly from the propaganda used in a democracy such as the United States. Although I believe that the categories could be applied universally with further study and exploration, I will deal solely with the American form of democracy to eliminate ambiguities.

Second, the examples chosen in this and the following chapters will be spoken or written from the President to the public. The categories are, therefore, from his point of view. Excerpts from a personal diary or conversations between the President and a single individual will not be used. Although propaganda can be used to target single individuals, it is most readily apparent and effective in public settings. As Jaques Ellul argues, "Propaganda is effective not when based on an individual prejudice, but when based on a collective center of interest, shared by the crowds."[116]   Examples will, therefore, consist of broad appeals or pleas to the public.

Positive Propaganda

When appealing to the American public, Presidents use positive forms of propaganda to help unify, integrate, or uplift the people. Its use involves an attempt to lower tension and anxiety -- to ease the minds of others. It closely parallels Jaques Ellul's notion of the propaganda of integration. As he suggests, "integration propaganda aims at stabilizing the

---

[116] *Propaganda: The Formation of Men's Attitudes,* 49.

social body, at unifying and reinforcing it."[117] It decreases the A-T level and is usually only used in cases where that level is already dangerously high; i.e., during times of war or internal strife. Often, positive propaganda seeks to dampen tension, to save the existing order; for, if the political or social situation becomes too explosive, revolutions or other upheavals could occur.

Positive propaganda is used to re-establish the individual within a collectivity. In other words, the propagandist hopes to create a sense of unity in order to surround the masses in an all-encompassing system of beliefs (ideology). To do this, positive emotions must be invoked. These emotions can include love, hope, pride, acceptance, and joy.[118] By appealing to positive emotions, anxiety and tension are decreased within the personality, thereby lowering the A-T level and creating a more stable environment. Positive propaganda:

> aims at making the individual participate in his society in every way. It is a long-term propaganda, a self-reproducing propaganda that seeks to obtain stable behavior, to adapt the individual to his everyday life, to reshape his thoughts and behavior in terms of the permanent social setting. We can see that this propaganda is more extensive and complex than propaganda of agitation. It must be permanent, for the individual can no longer be left to himself.[119]

In the last century, Presidents have used positive propaganda in different manners. As mentioned previously,

---

[117] Ibid, 75.

[118] See the list of primary emotions in Psychology: Themes and Variations, (Pacific Grove: Brooks/Cole Publishing Co., 1992) 367.

[119] *Propaganda: The Formation of Men's Attitudes,* 75.

it is often used in war-time situations. In the five major US conflicts of this century, World Wars I and II, the Korean War, Vietnam, and the Gulf War, positive propaganda has been used to lower the A-T level. It often acts as damage control. This is clearly evident in the propaganda used by Lyndon Johnson during the Vietnam War. In 1964, Johnson repeatedly used positive propaganda to disguise the escalating crisis in Vietnam. On October 21, 1964, he stated, "We are not going to send American boys nine or ten thousand miles away from home to do what Asian boys ought to be doing for themselves."[120] How can this be considered positive propaganda? It reassures the people that peace will be sought at all costs. This assurance could provoke any number of the aforementioned positive emotions. Six days later in a speech at Pittsburgh, Johnson reiterated this point: "There can be and will be, as long as I am President, peace for all Americans."[121] Even at the height of the war in 1968, Johnson still insisted that, "Our goal is peace and peace at the earliest possible moment."[122]

Why did Johnson use positive propaganda in this situation? Clearly, it served two purposes: first, to provide an optimistic outlook on a dismal situation, and second, to assure the people that Americans were fighting a worthwhile and winnable war. Johnson's rhetoric may have eased some of the tension present in the unstable political and social environment of the 60s. By reiterating that he desired peace, some of the mounting political pressure placed upon the President was relieved, even amidst the thousands of US casualties and protest movements. All positive statements by Johnson in speeches were not only directed to his immediate audience, but also the American public as well as

---

[120] Alfred Steinberg, Sam Johnson's Boy, (New York: Macmillan, 1968) 767.

[121] Eric F. Goldman, The Tragedy of Lyndon Johnson, (New York: Alfred A. Knopf, 1969) 412.

[122] Taken from his fifth State of the Union address -- James David Barber, Presidential Character, (Englewood Cliffs: Prentice Hall, 1992) 27.

international observers. Regardless of whether or not he truly desired peace, Johnson used positive propaganda to alleviate some of the tension created by war.[123]

In the Gulf War, President George Bush used similar techniques to assure the American public. With the crisis in the Middle East escalating, Bush deployed 500,000 soldiers. Although dissent remained minimal, Bush discussed America's role in a New World Order to justify American involvement in the Gulf. In his State of the Union address, Bush stated: "We are engaged in a great struggle in the skies and on the seas and sands. We know why we're there; We are Americans part of something larger than ourselves."[124]He was referring to America "as an inspiring example of freedom and democracy,"[125]-- a guidepost for the post-Cold War era. This speech targeted the positive emotions of pride which could then be used to legitimate Gulf War action. By evoking pride, President Bush decreased the A-T level.

Positive propaganda is also used by the Presidents in times of domestic upheaval. To demonstrate its use, three examples will be used: President Eisenhower's rhetoric in the Little Rock crisis, President Carter's handling of the Iranian hostage situation, and President Hoover's statements during the Great Depression. Although the outcomes differed, in all instances, positive propaganda was used to lower the A-T level, and attempts were made to reassure the public.

---

[123] Was Johnson's use of positive propaganda successful? I would argue that it had some effect. With the A-T level at a dangerously high level, propaganda can only do so much. Propaganda is best utilized in situations where pressures are building but not at a crisis point. For example, Johnson's use of propaganda in 1964 was more effective than in 1968. Further studies should be done to determine the true effect of the function of propaganda.

[124] George Bush, "Address before a Joint Session of the Congress on the State of the Union, January 29, 1991," *Weekly Compilation* (1991), 90.

[125] Ibid, 91.

On September 23, 1957, President Eisenhower sent federal troops to Little Rock, Arkansas to enforce desegregation laws. At a time of extreme polarization between blacks and whites, this move by the President could have easily sparked riots or mobs of unruly citizens. Eisenhower, realizing the explosiveness of the situation and "challenge" to "the position of the Presidency,"[126] addressed the public through a September 21 statement:

the local law enforcement agencies have announced that they are prepared to maintain law and order...the sincere and conscientious efforts of the citizens of Little Rock prior to September second show that they are persons of good will who feel a responsibility to preserve and respect the law -- whether or not they personally agree with it. I am confident that they will vigorously oppose any violence by extremists.[127]

In this statement, the President appeals to several positive emotions at once -- love for others, respect of the law, pride and confidence in the good judgment of the people, and so on.

When the crisis actually occurs, Eisenhower once again plays the role of the father-figure. He assures the public with remarks stating that United States laws will be executed even if it requires him to "use the full power of the United States including whatever force may be necessary to prevent any obstruction of the law."[128] With the proper use of

---

[126] Richard Neustadt, *Presidential Power*, (New York, John Wiley and Sons, 1960) 31.

[127] "Statement by the President," *Hagerty Papers*, Box 6, "Integration -- Little Rock, 1957," Eisenhower Library taken from Martin J. Medhurst, *The Modern Presidency and Crisis Rhetoric*, (Westport: Praeger, 1994) 32.

[128] Dwight Eisenhower, "Statement by the President Regarding Occurrences at Central High School in Little Rock," *Public Papers*, 689.

propaganda coupled by federal force, Eisenhower demonstrated that he was both fox and lion.

Jimmy Carter, on the other hand, never truly mastered the art of persuasion. This is exemplified in his handling of the Iranian hostage crisis of 1979. On November 4, in response to the US detainment of the former Shah, several Iranians attacked the US embassy in Tehran taking 50 to 60 hostages. The situation quickly escalated, and as Amos Kiewe suggests, "President Carter's public responses to the situation in Iran quickly transformed the events surrounding the hostages into a crisis of character -- a test of his and the American public's compassion, unity, and fortitude."[129]Carter responded to the situation using positive propaganda. He declared:

> No act has so galvanized the American public toward unity in the last decade as has the holding of our people as hostages in Tehran. We stand today as one people. We are dedicated to the principles and the honor of our Nation.

Here, the unifying aspects of positive propaganda can be seen. The President attempts to integrate the citizenry into one group - "We stand today as one people." On November 28 at a news conference, Carter continued his use of positive propaganda: "During these past days our national will, our courage, and our maturity have all been severely tested, and history will show that the people of the United States have met every test."[130] Once again, he invokes the positive emotions of national pride.

---

[129] Amos Kiewe, *The Modern Presidency and Crisis Rhetoric*, (Westport: Praeger Series in Political Communication, 1994) 143.
[130] Jimmy Carter, "The President's News Conference of November 28, 1979," *Public Papers*, 2169.

Probably the best example of the use of positive propaganda in a crisis situation is that of Herbert Hoover's attempts to calm the public during the Great Depression.[131] Lacking the showmanship of other Presidents, Hoover often relied on facts to support his claim. Eugene Lyons suggests that this was one of his downfalls:

The presidency is very much of a showman's job. Leadership from the White House must appeal to the heart no less than to the mind; it must arouse faith and fervor and courage beyond cold calculations. In insisting that it was not a showman's job, Hoover was rationalizing his distaste for showmanship and his ineptitude behind the footlights.

Throughout the Great Depression, Hoover insisted that the economic situation was recovering or not affected at all by the slowdown. October 25, 1929, the day after "Black Thursday," the President said: "The fundamental business of the country, that is, the production and distribution of commodities, is on a very sound and prosperous basis...There has been a tendency for wage increases and the output per worker has increased, all of which indicates a very healthy situation."[132] These statements attempted to lower the A-T level by appealing to the positive emotions of hope and assurance.

As the economic conditions of the United States deteriorated, Hoover continued using positive propaganda. On December 3, 1929, he stated, "The country has enjoyed a large degree of prosperity and sound progress during the past year with a steady improvement in methods of production and distribution and consequent advancement in

[131] Eugene Lyons, *Our Unknown Ex-President: A Portrait of Herbert Hoover* (Garden City: Doubleday, 1948) 29.
[132] Herbert Hoover, "The President's News Conference of October 25, 1929," Public Papers, 355.

standards of living."[133]   The following year, on March 7, 1930, Hoover suggested that in early May citizens can look forward to "the amelioration of seasonal unemployment, the gaining strength of other forces, and the continued cooperation of the many agencies actively cooperating with the Government to restore business and to relieve distress."[134]   This positive rhetoric continued throughout Hoover's tenure and was probably largely ineffective. It was impossible to convince Americans that things are getting better while 25% of them lack employment.

Given that the purpose of positive propaganda is to lower the A-T level, it is most often used in crisis situations. But this does not preclude the use of positive propaganda in the absence of internal or external strife. In Bill Clinton's inaugural address several positive images were presented, among them this glorification of the American will and spirit:

> Today we do more than celebrate America, we rededicate ourselves to the very idea of America: an idea born in revolution and renewed through two centuries of challenge; an idea tempered by the knowledge that, but for fate, we -- the fortunate and the unfortunate -- might have been each other; and idea ennobled by the faith that our nation can summon from its myriad diversity the deepest measure of unity; an idea infused with the conviction that America's long, heroic journey must go forever upward.[135]

[133]   Ibid, 411.

[134]   Herbert Hoover, "Statement on Unemployment and Business Conditions. March 7, 1930," *Public Papers*, 78.

[135]   Gerald M. Pomper, *The Election of 1992*, (Chantham: Chatham House Publishers, 1993) 222.

Regardless of its use, positive propaganda seeks change through lowering the A-T level.

Negative Propaganda

Propaganda is usually interpreted to mean any open attempt to convince others or move them to action. This older definition incorporates the use of propaganda in war time situations. In fact, many are reminded of the infamous "propaganda teams", i.e., Wilson and Creel or Hitler and Goebbels. As Alfred Lee suggests, the people have "remembered how George Creel, America's wartime director of propaganda, oversold the 'war to end all wars,' the 'war to make the world safe for democracy.' And they remembered how atrocity stories...were exposed and how this tended to discredit all high-pressure propaganda for nationalism and war."[136] Propaganda, in this sense, is seen as negative in its usage and is more visible or more readily identified by the people. How does this differ from the new propaganda definition? The more modern propaganda utilizes Machiavellian tactics to conceal itself and its motives. It does not necessarily have to be used for negative reasons as was demonstrated in the previous section.

What, then, is this modern negative propaganda? Negative propaganda is the appeal to negative emotive values to increase the Anxiety-Tension level in personalities. Through its usage, it evokes one or more of the following negative emotions: fear, anger, disgust, contempt, shame,

---

[136] Alfred McClung Lee, *How to Understand Propaganda*, (New York: Rinehart and Co., Inc., 1953) 22.

and distress.[137] In *Propaganda: The Formation of Men's Attitudes*, Jaques Ellul recognizes this form of manipulation and labels it the propaganda of agitation. As was stated previously, it is most closely associated with war, protests, and rebellions. It "addresses itself...to internal elements in each of us, but it is always translated into reality by physical involvement in a tense and overexcited activity."[138] By causing tension to rise, the leader can incite action. In other words, it fans the flames of discontent and "unleashes an explosive movement"[139] towards change.

The modern Presidency uses negative propaganda incessantly. Presidents have, however, adapted it to their own needs. For example, negative propaganda is not only used in times of war and other crises but also to bash opponents or critics. Because Presidential power is limited, the President must rely on persuasive tactics: "The President has so few powers available to him, many of which are usable at only high costs; so he has no alternative but to try to persuade government players and convince them that what they want is what he wants."[140] Derogatory statements are often used to discredit the claims of an enemy, but the President must be focused and selective in his use of negative propaganda. As Mencius suggested, "One who aims at too many goals will not only disquiet his mind, but may even fail to achieve any of them."[141] In the following paragraphs, I will examine two uses of negative propaganda: (1) its use in crisis situations and (2) its use against critics.

---

[137] Based on Silvan Tomkins list of primary emotions. See *Psychology: Themes and Variations*, 367.

[138] *Propaganda: Formation of Men's Attitudes*, 72.

[139] Ibid, 72.

[140] Interview with Richard Neustadt at 2:35 pm on October 26, 1995.

[141] Creel, H.G., *Chinese Thought from Confucius to Mao Tse-tung*, (New York: Mentor Book, 1953) 78.

Both in World Wars I and II, negative propaganda was used continually to foster hostility in the American public towards the enemy. Woodrow Wilson with the assistance of George Creel became renowned for using these tactics. He implied that the German government had "put aside all restraints of law or of humanity."[142] Using his moralist and sometimes elitist rhetoric, he painted a hideous picture of the enemy. Germany's ingenious use of submarines to destroy Allied supply ships was described by Wilson as "warfare against mankind."[143] Throughout the war, Wilson continued to bombard the American public with propaganda. Although the majority of the methods used involved colorful phrasing or exaggerated stories, Wilson had no qualms about lying to further his goals. In 1917, the President used the Zimmerman note to raise tension. This fabricated letter suggested that the Germans attempted to form a military alliance with Mexico which threatened the United States. Wilson argued: "That it [the German government] means to stir up enemies against us at our very doors the intercepted note to the German Minister at Mexico City is eloquent evidence."[144] Wilsons's rhetoric, when it was effective, appealed to the gamut of negative emotions from anger to fear. This propaganda raised A-T levels, and as a result, kept war morale high.

Franklin D. Roosevelt used similar methods during World War II. After the bombing of Pearl Harbor in 1941, Roosevelt addressed Congress with the "Day of Infamy" speech. In it, he used negative propaganda to raise the A-T level for two reasons: (1) to gain public support and (2) to

---

[142] Karlyn Kohrs Campbell and Kathleen Hall Jamieson, *Deeds Done in Words,* (Chicago: The University of Chicago Press, 1990) 108.
[143] Ibid, 109.
[144] Ibid, 121.

convince Congress of the necessity of declaring war.[145] On December 8, 1941 he stated:

> Yesterday, December 7, 1941 -- a date which will live in infamy -- the United States of America was suddenly and deliberately attacked by naval and air forces of the Empire of Japan...The attack yesterday on the Hawaiian Islands has caused severe damage to American naval and military forces. I regret to tell you that very many Americans lives have been lost. In addition, American ships have been reported torpedoes on the high seas between San Franciso and Honolulu. Yesterday the Japanese Government also launched an attack against Malaya. Last night Japanese forces attacked Hong Kong. Last night Japanese forces attacked Guam. Last night Japanese forces attacked the Philippine Islands. Last night the Japanese attacked Wake Island. And this morning the Japanese attacked Midway Island...The facts of yesterday and today speak for themselves.[146]

I chose to quote this particular speech at length to illustrate the methods used by Roosevelt to create tension. Although this study does not deal directly with the techniques of propaganda, I feel that the reader would benefit from a more in-depth analysis to understand the composition of propaganda. Roosevelt uses several stylistic approaches -- the most obvious being the repetition of "Last

---

[145] Roosevelt's desire to enter the war is well-documented. He used this event as the single match which would ignite the bonfire of events to come.

[146] Franklin Roosevelt, "Address to Congress Asking that a State of War Be Declared Between the United States and Japan. December 8, 1941," *Public Papers*, 514-515.

night the Japanese attacked..." This pounds an image into Roosevelt's audience (the Congress but also the public) and implies that Japan is militarily capable of causing vast damage to the United States. This, in turn, creates the negative emotion of distress. Roosevelt also appeals to anger when he mentions the large number of causalities and losses to the naval fleet. But above all, the President's speech elicits fear. America has been attacked for the first time in many years, many of their soldiers died at Pearl Harbor, and the world is at war. Fear is already present and Congress needed little convincing, but Roosevelt, seizing the moment, uses propaganda to have war declared.

The second use of negative propaganda that I will examine involves the lambasting of opponents. In a two party, three branch system, conflict is bound to occur. As Ginsberg and Shefter suggest, "Institutional combat of the sort that has characterized American politics in recent years is most likely to occur when the major branches of government are controlled by hostile forces."[147] Although the attacks of negative propaganda are directed at the opponents, the purpose of its use is to cause the A-T level to increase in the masses. It must also be noted that the effectiveness of negative propaganda can vary tremendously from being completely ineffective to causing rapid change.[148]

Franklin Roosevelt used negative propaganda to criticize political factions threatening his own goals. On January 11, 1944 in the State of the Union address, Roosevelt stated:

---

[147] Benjamin Ginsberg and Martin Shefter, *Politics by Other Means*, (US: Basic Books, 1990) 17-18.

[148] To analyze the effectiveness of negative or any form of propaganda would involve using methods similar to those used to gauge public opinion. This paper will not discuss this issue but further studies should be done to determine the correlation if any between propaganda and end result.

The overwhelming majority of our people have met the demands of this war...However, while the majority goes on about its great work without complaint, a noisy minority maintains an uproar of demands for special favors for special groups. There are pests who swarm through the lobbies of the Congress and the cocktail bars of Washington, representing these special groups as opposed to the basic interests of the Nation as a whole...Such selfish agitation can be highly dangerous in wartime. It creates confusion. It damages morale. It hampers our national effort. It muddies the waters and therefore prolongs the war.[149]

Once again Roosevelt demonstrates his manipulative talents. In this excerpt, he does three essential things. First, he implies that his critics are nothing more than lazy complainers; second, he suggests that if these special groups are not silenced the war will be prolonged; third he recognizes his opponents as a destabilizing force. How do these things affect the A-T level? They cause tension to increase and surface in the form of negative emotions such as contempt or anger towards the special groups, or distress over the war continuing.

A second example can be seen in Richard Nixon's attempt to place a limit of $250 billion on government spending in 1973. Nixon bickered constantly with Congress over this issue and the mud-slinging began. In a radio message, he said, "The Congress suffers from institutional faults when it comes to federal spending...Congress not only does not consider the total financial picture when it votes on

[149] Franklin Roosevelt, "Message on the State of the Union. January 11, 1944," *Public Papers*, 34-35.

a particular spending bill, it does not even contain a mechanism to do so if it wished."[150]

Clearly this example is stereotyping propaganda which will be discussed in the next chapter, but it also acts as negative propaganda. Although more mild in its approach, it seeks to raise the A-T level by directing attacks at Congress. Congress, in turn, responded with more negative statements which also increase the A-T level. This form of negative propaganda basically affects tension and anxiety in general. It may provoke specific emotions such as anger towards one of the political actors but in general the instability caused with the arguments raises the A-T level. As Jaques Ellul argues, stability and adjustment are the goals of all individuals: "people have come to realize that a group in which conflicts, recriminations, and jealousies between individuals abound is not only a less happy group...but also a group much less efficient in the performance of a task or the fulfillment of a function."[151] Negative propaganda, therefore, places pressure on opponents to resolve conflict and seek stability.

Satisficing Propaganda

The third and final function of propaganda involves maintaining the status quo. Often, the President may be content with the current political situation and desires to keep things the way they are. In order to do this, he can use satisficing propaganda. The term "satisficing" was developed by Herbert A. Simon throughout his works. In an article in Psychological Review, Simon explained his idea of

---

[150] William S. Livinston, Lawrence C. Dodd, and Richard L. Schott, *The Presidency and the Congress*, (Austin: The University of Texas, 1979) 102.
[151] *The Political Illusion*, 206-207.

a person's desire to satisfice. He suggested that when faced with multiple options, the individual will choose an option which fulfills the basic requirements of his goals instead of an optimal path: "Evidently, organisms adapt well enough to 'satisfice'; they do not, in general, 'optimize.'"[152] In other words, humans and other organisms are satisfied with "finding a course of action that is 'good enough.'"[153] Simon questions the maximizing assumption most theorists assume when discussing economics or social science; that is, a person will naturally search for the option which not only fulfills his basic requirements, but is also the best option available -- "Most human decision-making, whether individual or organizational, is concerned with the discovery and selection of satisfactory alternatives; only in exceptional cases is it concerned with the discovery and selection of optimal alternatives."[154]

Propaganda, when used to satisfice, is done merely to keep the populace content with the status quo. It does not directly seek to increase or decrease the A-T level but to maintain the present state. Satisficing propaganda is used frequently by every President in almost every situation. In fact, it is used so frequently that it becomes difficult to distinguish from the President's regular rhetoric. In the following paragraphs, several examples will be given to illustrate the use of satisficing propaganda.

Presidents who were relatively inactive in office used satisficing propaganda in many situations. President Harding, for example, in his tenure followed the "normal

---

[152] Herbert A. Simon, "Rational Choice and the Structure of the Environment," *Psychological Review*, (vol. 63, no. 2, 1956) 129.

[153] Herbert A. Simon, *Models of Man*, (London: Chapman and Hall, Ltd., 1957) 205.

[154] Herbert A. Simon, *Organizations*, (New York: John Wiley and Sons, Inc., 1958) 140-141.

procedure, the natural way, without excess."[155] William Howard Taft provides another excellent example. As Erwin Hargrove suggests, Taft and the other Presidents of Restraint "did not put a high value on personal or Presidential power, and in the course of their careers they did not develop political skills."[156] The use of satisficing propaganda was probably not a conscious effort on the part of Taft but simply reflected his inaptitude at using Presidential persuasion.

In a speech given on January 15, 1909, Taft demonstrated his inability to use more dynamic forms of propaganda. He stated:

> I am a Republican, but I concede fully the great advantages to the country in having a Democratic party sufficiently powerful sometimes to win the Presidential elections and always to put the Republican party when in control in fear of a possible or probable defeat.[157]

Compare this to President Wilson's thrashing of his Republican opponents in Congress who opposed the League of Nations:

> I am not one of those that have the least anxiety about the triumph of the principles I have stood for...I have seen fools resist Providence before and I have seen their destruction, as will come upon these again -- utter destruction and contempt.[158]

---

[155] Robert K. Murray, *The Politics of Normalcy: Governmental Theory and Practice in the Harding-Coolidge Era*, (New York: W.W. Norton, 1973) 43.

[156] Erwin C. Hargrove, *Presidential Leadership: Personality and Political Style*, (New York: MacMillan, 1966) 1.

[157] William H. Taft, *Political Issues and Outlooks*, (New York: Doubleday, Page and Company, 1909) 234.

[158] Alexander L. and Juliette L. *George, Woodrow Wilson and Colonel House*, (New York: John Day, 1956) 314.

The second example clearly uses harsher language and stereotyping propaganda to present a negative image of Republicans. The first example is more satisficing. It does not seek to alter the attitudes toward the given subject but to maintain the current outlook. Taft's statement is also lacking the prejudicial and biased tones present in Wilson's declaration. Clearly, Taft did not want to alter the A-T level by supporting or criticizing the opposing party.

Presidents who are active in office also use satisficing propaganda to maintain the present A-T level. President Theodore Roosevelt's speech on January 4, 1904 illustrates this point. In it, he began by using satisficing propaganda:

> By the said act the President was authorized to secure for the United States the property of the Panama Canal Company and the perpetual control of a strip six miles wide across the Isthmus of Panama...The language quoted defines with exactness and precision what was to be done, and what as a matter of fact has been done...control has now been obtained; the provision of the act has been complied with; it is no longer possible under existing legislation to go to the Nicaragua route as an alternative.[159]

In the preceding statement, facts are presented and no true propaganda attempt is made. Roosevelt, following the provisions established in a 1902 Act, is informing Congress of the action that will be taken. However, Roosevelt also uses negative propaganda when discussing the Panama

---

[159] Theodore Roosevelt, *Addresses and Messages*, (New York: G.P. Putnam's Sons, 1904) 427.

Canal. He wanted to raise the A-T level in the members of Congress so that action would be taken:

> The United States thus assumed the position of guarantor of the canal and of its peaceful use by all the world. The guaranty included as a matter of course the building of the canal. The enterprise was recognized as responding to an international need; and it would be the veriest travesty on right and justice to treat the governments in possession of the Isthmus as having the right, in the language of Mr. Cass, ' to close the gate of intercourse on the great highways of the world, and justify the act by the pretension that these avenues of trade and travel belong to them and that they choose to shut them.[160]

Satisficing propaganda is, therefore, used to stabilize and support the present order. Only when change or action must be taken immediately is positive or negative propaganda used.

This chapter has answered the question, "What does propaganda hope to accomplish?" It has demonstrated the function of propaganda by illustrating its effect on the A-T level in personalities. The next chapter will examine the types of propaganda available to the President and answer the question, "How is propaganda used?"

---

[160] Ibid, 429.

Chapter Four:

Propaganda and Its Use

In the previous chapter, propaganda's ability to manipulate key aspects of the personality was explored. Three forms of propaganda (positive, negative, and satisficing) were discussed, but these categories do not address the forms of propaganda used to elicit a certain result. In other words, the groupings do not answer the question, "How is propaganda used by the leader?" As Jaques Ellul argues, propaganda is "designed to transform certain values, to modify current concepts, to provoke psychological twists in the individual."[161] Harold Lasswell suggests that there are three core values -- income, safety, and deference -- that can be manipulated by the propagandist to evoke a specific reaction. In Propaganda Technique in the World War, Lasswell argues that, "the achievements of propaganda are affected by the traditional prejudices of the nation and of each constituent group."[162] In other words, if the leader is to be successful, he must appeal to the values of the target group.

How does the leader manipulate these values? The modern president can appeal to values in four different ways. First, the leader can appeal to ideological or sociological values in a vague manner where there is no attempt to define

---

[161] *Propaganda: Formation of Men's Attitudes*, 60.
[162] *Propaganda Technique in the World War*, 185.

or re-define a specific value (symbolic). A second form involves the selective interpretation of one or more values. The propagandist attempts to manipulate one group of values over other values in order to persuade (selective). Third, the President can reinforce certain values or beliefs in individuals. In doing so, other values are also down played or attacked(stereotyping). The fourth and final form of propaganda calls upon values of either the past or the future to incite action to attain those values. The President evokes certain values which are not present in the current system to persuade the masses (visionary). The following paragraphs will explore these different forms of propaganda using examples from the modern Presidency as evidence.

Symbolic Propaganda

Propaganda can be simple or complex in nature depending on the form used (see fig. 4.1).

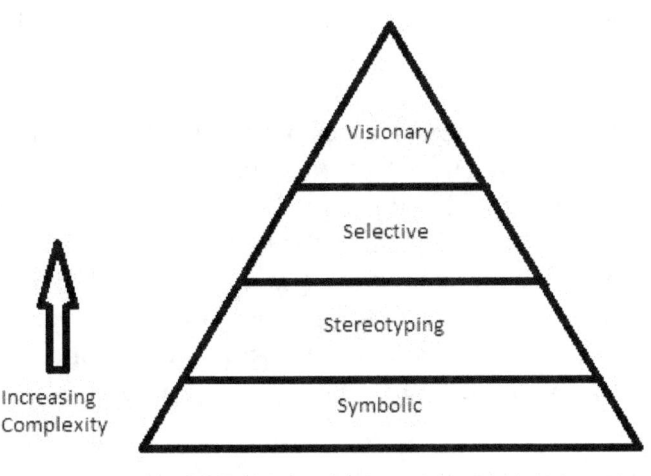

Complexity and Types of Propaganda
Fig. 4.1

As the most basic form, symbolic propaganda attempts to identify with the values or core beliefs that are already present in society. Values obviously differ from person to person and over time, but there are certain values ingrained in the majority of individuals through the process of political socialization. They are the values that help individuals justify their lives and their existence, that create an all-encompassing image which is "aimed at obtaining adherence to a society, its principles, its ideology, and its myths -- and to the behavior required by authorities."[163]

Symbolic propaganda does not necessarily seek to agitate or change the opinions of others. It is a response to a need generated by the masses. They desire complacency and search for explanations to make their life meaningful. Jaques Ellul argues that modernity and technological innovations have created an apathetic world fueled by propaganda. In order to survive mentally in this world, individuals must convince themselves that they can maintain a certain degree of humanity; that they are still essentially more important than computers and technology. Propaganda helps them to perform this task. As Ellul suggests:

> One can lead a horse to water but cannot make him drink; one cannot reach through propaganda those who do not need what it offers. The propagandee is by no means just an innocent victim. He provokes the psychological action of propaganda, and not merely lends himself to it. but even derives satisfaction from it. Without this previous, implicit consent, without this need for propaganda

---

[163] *Propaganda: Formation of Men's Attitudes*, 83.

experienced by practically every citizen of the technological age, propaganda could not spread.[164]

These values, then, are the values shared by the majority of individuals within a regime. As Samuel Huntington argues, "For the United States these are liberty, democracy, equality, private property, and markets."[165] For example, in America, freedom of speech and other values encompassed by the Bill of Rights are believed to be basic rights. Symbolic propaganda does not even have to appeal to a certain value but the symbols associated with these values -- "the single executive image rests on symbolism -- the president symbolizes the nation, its people, and its government. There is a symbolic equivalence between the president and the public, with the blurring together as one in presidents' speeches and in media coverage of the office."[166] For example, posters of Uncle Sam, the American eagle, and the White House are all symbols of ideals fostered by propaganda. We are constantly bombarded with symbolic propaganda. It is simple, effusive, and effective. It reassures and simplifies. It is the "motherhood, apple pie, and early spring" appeal. Without this barrage of propaganda, democracy could not succeed.

Symbolic propaganda is similar to Donald Stokes' notion of valence issues in politics. Valence issues are those topics in "which there is essentially one body of opinion on values or goals."[167] They differ from what he calls position issues which are marked by a diversity of opinions. How do

[164]   Ibid, 121.

[165]   Samuel Huntington, "Why International Primacy Matters," *The Cold War and After: Prospects for Peace*, (London: MIT Press, 1993) 321.

[166]   Lyn Ragsdale, "Studying the Presidency: Why Presidents Need Political Scientists," *The Presidency and the Political System*, (Washington, D.C.: Congressional Quarterly Press, 1995) 42.

[167]   David Butler and David Stokes, *Political Change in Britain: The Evolution of Electoral Change*, (New York: St. Martin's Press, 1974) 292.

leaders use valence issues in campaigns? Political parties "mount their appeals by choosing from a larger set of potential valence issues those on which their identification with positive symbols and their opponents' with negative symbols will be most to their advantage."[168] By choosing the same "goals or symbols of which almost everyone approves or disapproves,"[169] the leader can effectively manipulate the public.

Murray Edelman echoes Stokes' ideas in The Symbolic Uses of Politics. He refers to the unimodal value structure "which the American population has most closely conformed through most of United States history."[170] This matrix of core beliefs spreads throughout the populace and creates a general consensus on certain issues. Politicians tap into these values to gain public support. As Edelman suggests, "There can be open and dramatic appeals for public support, for the support is already great and the likelihood of massive opposition to basic policies slight."[171] By calling upon a unimodal value, similar responses are elicited from all members of the audience which provides for predictability and effective propaganda.

The leader often tries to create a favorable impression by evoking ideological or sociological symbols. For example, Harry Truman in a speech given on April 16, 1945 used symbolic propaganda to bolster the morale of the people. With the continuance of World War II in the Pacific as well as the death of Franklin Roosevelt, many citizens had little confidence in an unproven vice-president as their leader. In this speech, Truman states:

---

[168] Donald Stokes, "Valence Politics," *Electoral Politics*, (Oxford: Clarendon Press, 1992) 146.

[169] Ibid, 143.

[170] Murray Edelman, *The Symbolic Uses of Politics*, (Urbana: University of Illinois Press, 1964) 176.

[171] Ibid, 176.

Here in America, we have labored long and hard to achieve a social order worthy of our great heritage. In our time, tremendous progress has been made toward a really democratic way of life. Let measure the foreword-looking people of America that there will be no relaxation in our efforts to improve the common lot of the people...On the battlefields, we have frequently faced overwhelming odds -- and won! At home, Americans will not be less resolute! We shall never cease our struggle to preserve and maintain our American way of life.[172]

Truman is appealing to several symbolic values: the idea that Americans can overcome even in the face of "overwhelming odds", the "democratic way of life", and the American "heritage."[173]

A second and more noteworthy example of the use of symbolic propaganda appears in John F. Kennedy's inaugural address:

We dare not forget today that we are the heirs of that first revolution. Let the word go forth from this time and place, to friend and foe alike, that the torch has been passed to a new generation of Americans -- born in this century, tempered by war, disciplined by a hard and bitter peace, proud of our ancient heritage...let every nation know, whether it wishes us well or ill, that we shall pay any price, bear any burden, meet any hardship, support any friend,

[172] Harry S. Truman, "Address Before a Joint Session of the Congress. April 16, 1945," *Public Papers*, 3.

[173] Note that in the first two line of this quote, Truman could also be evoking values such as the Protestant work ethic or even Puritanical moral values ("social order").

oppose any foe to assure the survival and the success of liberty...And so, my fellow Americans: ask not what your country can do for you, but what you can do for your country. My fellow citizens of the world: ask not what America will do for you, but what together we can do for the freedom of the world.[174]

In his address, the President makes reference to several all-American values such as the "ancient heritage" of Americans and the "success of liberty." His use of symbolic propaganda is, however, more than just rhetoric. It inspires the audience and builds them up to the climatic point that calls for action -- "ask not what your country can do for you, but what you can do for your country."

A third and final example of symbolic propaganda can be seen in a speech Gerald Ford made on August 9, 1974 shortly after Richard Nixon's resignation. In it, he echoes the words of past Presidents by recalling the history of our government -- "Our Constitution works; our great Republic is a government of laws and not of men. Here the people rule."[175] He also alludes to the Christian tradition -- "But there is a higher Power, by whatever name we honor Him, who ordains not only righteousness but love, not only justice but mercy."[176] Ford's use of symbolic propaganda attempts to tap into the core values of the American lifestyle. Through it, he is better able to reassure and placate the fears of a populace faced with the trauma of Nixon's actions.

---

[174] John F. Kennedy, "Inaugural Address, April 16, 1995," *Public Papers*, 1-3.

[175] Gerald Ford, "Remarks on Taking Office, August 9, 1974," *Public Papers*, 2.

[176] Ibid, 2.

Selective Propaganda

Unlike symbolic propaganda, selective propaganda involves the manipulation or careful interpretation of one or more sociological or ideological values to persuade. In our own political system, values are construed in a variety of different ways. Equality, for example, can be used by both those who are for or against affirmative action. Individuals who support affirmative action may argue through the use of selective propaganda that in order to assure equality in the market place, measures must be taken to help minorities. In turn, those who are against affirmative action could argue that giving minorities an advantage over others is far from equal.[177] In this way, politicians have used beliefs and values to persuade others.

The Presidents have used selective propaganda in a variety of different ways. During the Great Depression, Herbert Hoover used selective propaganda continuously. As Harris Gaylord Warren suggests, "Hoover clung with wonderful stubbornness to the idea that local resources should be able to take care of hunger and misery regardless of their causes."[178] He, therefore, placed more emphasis on this value, the value of self-help or "rugged individualism", over others such as the belief in federal assistance to solve the economic crisis. Hoover argued that "economic depression cannot be cured by legislative action or executive pronouncement...each community and each State should

---

[177] Richard Ellis discusses the different meanings of equality used in our society and differentiates between equality of process and equality of result. Equality of process allows every individual to pursue his or her desired goals in the system. Equality of result suggests that all who compete in the race should receive the same reward or to a lesser extent equal work should equal pay. Richard J. Ellis, *American Political Cultures*, (New York: Oxford University Press, 1993) 43-62.

[178] Harris Gaylord Warren, *Herbert Hoover and the Great Depression*, (New York: Norton, 1959) 182-183.

assume its full responsibilities for organization of employment and relief of distress with that sturdiness and independence which built a great nation."[179]

Selective propaganda also served to bolster support for the Voting Rights Act of 1965. Lyndon Johnson in a speech given on March 15, 1965 addressed the right held by all citizens to have an equal voice in government. He argued that the purpose of the Act was "to right wrong, to do justice, and serve man."[180] By doing so, he appealed to these core values to identify with the American public. Throughout the speech, references are made to American ideals:

> The most basic right of all was the right to choose your own leaders. The history of this country, in large measure, is the history of the expansion of that right to all of our people...Every American citizen must have an equal right to vote. There is no reason which can excuse the denial of that right. There is no duty which weighs more heavily on us than the duty we have to ensure that right.[181]

Johnson implies that the most important right and liberty Americans have is the right to vote. In a different context, freedom of speech or religion might be advocated as the primary right of all citizens. The significance of Johnson's use of propaganda is that the value was selected to help pass this particular piece of legislation.

President Carter used selective propaganda in his inaugural address. In it, he stated, "In this outward and physical ceremony, we attest once again to the inner and

---

[179] Ibid, 193.

[180] James R. Andrews and David Zarefsky, *Contemporary American Voices*, (New York: Longman, 1992) 94.

[181] Ibid, 95.

spiritual strength of our Nation,"[182] suggesting that the inauguration ceremony is a sign of America's vigor. "Inner and spiritual strength" was chosen as the value advocated rather than other American ideals. Similarly, Franklin Roosevelt in his second inaugural address utilized selective propaganda to call for a return to the role of government as caretaker:

> Instinctively we recognize a deeper need -- the need to find through government the instrument of our united purpose to solve for the individual the ever-rising problems of a complex civilization...The essential democracy of our Nation and the safety of our people depend not upon the absence of power, but upon lodging it with those whom the people can change or continue at stated intervals through an honest and free system of elections.[183]

A final example of selective propaganda can be seen in Franklin D. Roosevelt's speech on April 26, 1939. In it, he asked for fair hiring practices echoing the words of the modern day advocates of affirmative action:

> As industry and business make substantial progress toward recovery there are ever-increasing employment opportunities for all groups. It is important to our social equilibrium that these opportunities be equitably shared, and that no group in the population shall feel itself discriminated against in hiring policies. It is particularly important that those men and women who have reached the age where their family responsibilities are at a peak receive their fair share of the new jobs, and are at

---

[182] Karlyn Kohrs Campbell and Kathleen Hall Jamieson, *Deeds Done in Words*, (Chicago: University of Chicago Press, 1990) 24.
[183] Ibid, 34.

least allowed to compete for these openings on the basis of their actual qualifications, freed from the handicap of an unfounded prejudice against age alone.[184]

At first glance, this passage appears to be a basic appeal to the American employer to hire out of work men and women, but a closer examination reveals use of propaganda designed to persuade the audience. First, Roosevelt uses selective propaganda by suggesting that equal employing practices are vital to our "social equilibrium" implying that without this form of equality society would somehow be in peril. He utilizes a second form of propaganda by arguing that those who do not hire based on age are "prejudiced" -- a term filled with negative connotations which adds to his selective use of equality in this speech. This form of propaganda will be examined in the next section.

Stereotyping Propaganda

Like selective propaganda, stereotyping propaganda seeks to support one set of values over another. There is, however, a difference on how the form of persuasion is used. In selective propaganda, one or several beliefs are used to incite action whether they be equality, justice, freedom, etc. No attempt is made to down play or degrade other values; those values are simply excluded from the statements of the leader. With stereotyping propaganda, the thoughts of citizens which are "narrowed to ideas and objects...through

---

[184] Franklin D. Roosevelt, " Employment Week and Employment Sunday. Proclamation No. 2331. April 26, 1939," *Public Papers*, 277.

propaganda"[185] are used to glorify certain ideals over others. By doing so, other values that differ from the ideological and sociological beliefs of the people are inevitably frowned upon by the public. Tony Harrison echoes these thoughts in his poem "Initial Illumination":

> let them remember, all those who celebrate,
> that their good news is someone else's bad[186]

Stereotyping propaganda relies on tapping into the predisposed beliefs which are present in a certain group and exploiting them through reinforcement of those values. However, unlike symbolic propaganda, the focus of stereotyping propaganda is very specific. It most closely mirrors Aristotle's idea of epideictic or oratorical rhetoric. As he suggests, "oratorical speeches either praise or blame people."[187]It identifies with a schema of prejudices, and through its use, discriminates against other values. Through this discrimination, certain beliefs are portrayed as the dominant values. Conversely, the values of others are viewed as inferior and either down played or attacked. Stereotyping propaganda is, therefore, "a weapon of direct attack upon...psychology."[188]

The use of stereotyping propaganda varies depending on its desired effect. It can be used in foreign policy against another nation, as the United States did with the Soviet Union in the Cold War, or in domestic politics, with one faction or group against another as seen with the

---

[185] Edward L. Bernays, *Propaganda*, (New York: Horace Liveright, 1928) 11.

[186] Tony Harrison, "Initial Illumination," taken from Kevin Robbins, "The War, the Screen, the Crazy Dog and Poor Mankind," *Media Culture and Society*, vol. 15, April 1993, 327.

[187] Aristotle, *Rhetoric found in Aristotle: Selected Works*, (Grinnel: The Peripatetic Press, 1991) 628.

[188] Harold D. Lasswell, Propaganda Technique in the World War, (New York: Alfred A. Knopf, 1927) 4.

Republicans and Democrats.[189]In the following paragraphs, examples of each will be explored.

Like negative propaganda, stereotyping propaganda is most apparent in war time situations. As a tool of foreign policy, it is used extensively. Because the leader is attacking an individual or group outside of the nation, it is easier to use, and the risk of upsetting factions within the country is decreased. As Harold Lasswell argues, it is one of the four "chief instruments of policy in war and peace."[190] During World War II, various persuasive techniques were used involving stereotyping propaganda. Posters, pamphlets, and the like were used to "dehumanize the enemy" and to fuel "existing racial prejudices by exaggerating stereotypes."[191] One popular technique involved "demeaning opponents through caricature."[192] Regardless of the form used, stereotyping propaganda was used to buttress domestic morale.

Lasswell also refers to stereotyping propaganda in a different context. In his final chapter of World Politics and Personal Insecurity, he discusses the "quest for a myth" -- a universal code which could be globally adopted. He argues that: "The prerequisite of a stable order in the world is a universal body of symbols and practices sustaining an elite which propagates itself by peaceful methods."[193] To maintain this "stable order," Lasswell suggests that leaders

---

[189] The use of any of these types of propaganda can be used both in foreign and domestic policy -- their influence on values remains the same. However, in order to illustrate the various uses of stereotyping propaganda, I felt an examination of both contexts was necessary.

[190] Harold D. Lasswell, "Political and Psychological Warfare," *Propaganda in War and Crisis*, (New York: George W. Stewart, 1951) 265. The other three instruments are economics, diplomacy, and arms.

[191] Catherine P. O'Keefe, "Powers of Persuasion," *Army*, vol. 44, January 1994, 31. A recent exhibit in the Circular Gallery in the National Archives displayed many of these posters.

[192] "Changing Sensibilities," *American History*, June 1995, 82.

[193] Harold Lasswell, *World Politics and Personal Insecurity*, (New York: Whittlesey House, 1935) 237.

will employ "effective social control."[194]These methods will include stereotyping propaganda -- "A new flame must burn out the canker of dissent and temper the steel of bellicose enthusiasm. The name of this new hammer and anvil of social solidarity is propaganda."[195]

President Truman used stereotyping propaganda during the Cold War. On December 15, 1950, Truman warned the nation of the Soviet threat. He suggested that this "menace of Communist aggression" was "'waging a relentless attack' against a 'lasting peace' sought by 'free nations,'" and that "this barbaric force was attempting to undermine, overwhelm, and employ 'threats and treachery and violence'...to 'push the world to the brink of a general war."[196] By doing so, Truman emphasized that the values of the United States as a "free nation" were the dominant values worth supporting and in turn, Soviet values, i.e. Communism, were at the same time debased. This lambasting of the U.S.S.R. during the Cold War served to support our own feelings of moral certitude.

President Reagan utilized similar methods. Throughout his tenure as President, Reagan referred to the

---

[194] Robert Horowitz, "Scientific Propaganda," *Essays on the Scientific Study of Politics*, (New York: Holt, Rinehart, and Winston, Inc., 1962) 274.

[195] *Propaganda Technique in the World War*, 221. Lasswell advocates the adoption of a new universal code which would primarily be based on his ideas of "psychoanalytocracy." If a new myth is going to develop, it could possibly be based on technology and capitalism. Francis Fukuyama addresses this issue and feels that the future will consist of a network of liberal capitalist regimes. Both Jaques Ellul and Herbert Marcuse also see the emerging dominance of technology and warn against it. These ideas will be discussed more thoroughly in chapter seven. *See* Francis Fukuyama, *The End of History and the Last Man*, (New York: Avon Books, 1992); Jaques Ellul, *Technological Society*, (New York: Vintage Books, 1964); Herbert Marcuse, *One-Dimensional Man*, (Boston: Beacon Press, 1964).

[196] Robert L. Ivie, "Declaring a National Emergency: Truman's Rhetorical Crisis and the Great Debate of 1951" *The Modern Presidency and Crisis Rhetoric*, (Westport: Praeger, 1994) 4.

Soviet Union as the "evil empire."[197] He used both negative and stereotyping propaganda to ingrain this unfavorable image in the minds of individuals. In a speech on June 11, 1982, Reagan stated that the "Soviet Union is engaged in the greatest military buildup in the history of the world," and that "it has used its new-found might to ruthlessly pursue its goals."[198]   Six days later he used more "evil empire" imagery:

> The decade of so-called detente witnessed the most massive Soviet buildup of military power in history...Soviet aggression and support for violence around the world have eroded the confidence needed for arms negotiations...Soviet oppression is not limited to the countries they invade. At the very time the Soviet Union is trying to manipulate the peace movement in the West, it is stifling a budding peace movement at home. In Moscow, banners are scuttled, buttons are snatched, and demonstrators are arrested when even a few people dare to speak about their fears.[199]

Clearly, Reagan enforced negative images of the Soviet Union through stereotyping propaganda. He also used this form of persuasion to reinforce American ideals. As Garry Wills argues, "He [Reagan] threw a geodesic dome of acronyms over all nations that would align themselves with America" referring to them as members of the "free

---

[197] "Asides: Empire's Evilness Affirmed," *Wall Street Journal* 3 Sep. 1991: A18.

[198] Ronald Reagan, "Remarks to the People of Berlin, June 11, 1982," *Public Papers*, 766.

[199] Ronald Reagan, "Remarks in New York City Before the United Nations General Assembly Special Session Devoted to Disarmament, June 17, 1982," *Public Papers*, 786.

world."[200] Stereotyping propaganda can also be used within nations against other factions or groups. Lyndon Johnson, for example, used stereotyping propaganda extensively during his tenure as President in response to critics of his actions in the Vietnam War. In a speech before Congress asking for an additional $700 million for the war effort, Johnson argued:

> For each member of Congress who supports this request is also voting to persist in our effort to halt Communist aggression in South Vietnam. Each is saying that the Congress and the President stand united before the world in joint determination that the independence of South Vietnam shall be preserved and the Communist attack will not succeed...Nothing will do more to strengthen your country in the world than the proof of national unity which an overwhelming vote for this appropriation will clearly show. To deny and delay the fullest support of the American people and the American Congress to those brave men who are risking their lives for freedom in Vietnam.[201]

In this passage, Johnson implies that those who do not vote for the appropriations will not only allow Communist aggression to persist, but will also be apathetic towards the "brave men who are risking their lives for freedom." In this manner, he is indirectly calling the members of Congress who do not support him cowards and tapping into the prejudices associated with such a label.

---

[200] Garry Wills, *Reagan's America*, (New York: Penguin Books, 1988) 419-420.

[201] Lyndon B. Johnson, *Public Papers*, 1965, 1: 494, 498; cited from *Deeds Done in Words*, 117-118.

A final example of stereotyping propaganda is visible in Woodrow Wilson's third State of the Union address given on December 7, 1915:

> There are citizens of the United States, I blush to admit, born under other flags but welcomed under our generous naturalization laws to the full freedom and opportunity of America, who have poured the poison of disloyalty into the very arteries of our national life; who have sought to bring the authority and good name of our Government into contempt, to destroy our poses to strike at them, and to debase our politics to the uses of foreign intrigue. There number is not great...but it is great enough to have brought deep disgrace upon us and to have made it necessary that we should promptly make use of processes of law by which we may be purged of their corrupt distempers.[202]

Here, Wilson insinuates that those who patronize a side in the "great European conflict" are a "deep disgrace," un-American, and desire war. They are, therefore, vilified, whereas those who do not favor a party in the war promote "the peace and dignity of the United States."[203]

[202] Woodrow Wilson, ed. Fred Israel, *The State of the Union Messages of the Presidents 1790-1966*, (New York: Chelsea House, 1966) 2571-2572.
[203] *Deeds Done in Words*, 56.

Visionary Propaganda

"I have a dream that one day this nation will rise up and live out the true meaning of its creed: "We hold these truths to be self-evident; that all men are created equal."[204]

-- Martin Luther King, Jr.

The speeches of Martin Luther King, Jr. epitomize the use of visionary propaganda in modern times. In the preceding quote, for example, he calls to a future filled with more harmony and equality for all races. If the President can call on either values in the near future or to values in the past, he can create hope and reassure individuals. By appealing to values used outside of the present time frame, the President can address the situation and provide an answer to the problem at hand.

Throughout time, political theorists have used visionary propaganda to create their utopias or answer the problems of an era. Adolf Hitler in Mein Kampf discussed a world which would benefit from ethnic cleansing. He argued, "racial purity, universally valid in Nature, is not only the sharp outward delimitation of the various races, but their uniform character in themselves,"[205] and in doing so, he used visionary propaganda to suggest that the Aryan race was supreme. The radical feminist, Monique Wittig, followed a similar line of reasoning. She argued that, "men are biologically inferior to women."[206] Given this, women should fight for the suppression of "men as a class" as well

---

[204] Martin Luther King, Jr., "I Have a Dream," *Contemporary American Voices*, 80.
[205] Adolf Hitler, *Mein Kampf*, found in *Dogmas and Dreams*, (Chatham: Chatham House Publishers, Inc., 1991) 463.
[206] Monique Wittig, *One Is Not Born a Woman*, found in *Dogmas and Dreams*, 531.

as "the destruction of heterosexuality."[207] She provides new values which her followers can pursue just as Karl Marx did in the Communist Manifesto or John Stuart Mill did in *On Liberty*.

The Presidents can use visionary propaganda in one of two ways. They can call upon values of the past or hope for certain values in the future. As was suggested in chapter one, a good example of recalling past ideals can be found in Robert N. Bellah's *Habits of the Heart*. In it, he argues that Americans should either return to the republican values of the past or reinforce the "biblical strand" present in the United States. One of these options would apparently assist in eliminating the "radical individualism" already present in America.[208] Another example involves the "Christian coalition" and the radical right with members such as Pat Buchanan and Pat Robertson. These politicians seek a return to the ideals of Christian morality in politics and carry their views to a host of issues including abortion.[209]Using propaganda to promote a better future can easily be seen in socialist or communist writings or any activist ideological work. In the following paragraphs, examples from the modern Presidency will be given to illustrate the use of visionary propaganda in the 20th century.

In his inaugural address, Richard Nixon used visionary propaganda invoking past values. He revealed a world in crisis which desperately needed a return to the standards before and during World War II. Nixon said that as Americans:

---

[207] Ibid, 533,534.

[208] Robert N. Bellah, *Habits of the Heart,* (New York: Harper and Row Publishers, 1985).

[209] *See* Michael Lienesch, *Redeeming America: Piety and Politics in the New Christian Right*, (Chapel Hill: University of North Carolina Press, 1993).

We find ourselves rich in goods, but ragged in spirit; reaching with magnificent precision for the moon, but falling into raucous discord on earth.

We are caught in war, wanting peace. We're torn by division, wanting unity. We see around us empty lives, wanting fulfillment. We see tasks that need doing, waiting for hands to do them.[210]

With the problem identified, Nixon suggests that Franklin Roosevelt faced and answered a similar situation with a "nation ravaged by depression and gripped in fear."[211] His use of visionary propaganda asked the people to not only re-examine but also adopt the values of the past.

Calvin Coolidge in his inaugural address also used visionary propaganda to glorify past values. As he suggested, "If we examine carefully what we have done, we can determine the more accurately what we can do."[212] In this speech, Coolidge discusses the "experiences" which have "enlarged our freedom" and "strengthened our independence."[213] These events include uniting as a conglomeration of unified states, destroying slavery, and Manifest Destiny. Coolidge calls on the values of these experiences to mold modern Americans and to imply that they are values worthy of emulation.

Visionary propaganda can also be used by pointing to values obtainable in the near future.[214] For example,

---

[210] Richard M. Nixon, "First Inaugural Address, January 20, 1969," *Contemporary American Voices*, 258.

[211] Ibid, 258.

[212] Calvin Coolidge, *Inaugural Addresses of the U.S. Presidents from Washington to Nixon*, (Washington, D.C.: U.S. Government, 1974) 216.

[213] Ibid, 216.

[214] John F. Kennedy's inaugural address is another example of visionary propaganda and demonstrates a point worth noting. It is possible for several types of propaganda to be included in the same speech and even the same

Warren Harding on March 4, 1921 stated, "Service is the supreme commitment of life. I would rejoice to acclaim the era of the Golden Rule and crown it with the autocracy of service."[215] Here, Harding acknowledges the worthwhile values associated with the Golden Rule and advocates a more service-oriented future.

Most Presidents have utilized visionary propaganda promising a better future in their domestic or economic programs. President Johnson used it to promote his Great Society. In a speech on May 22, 1964, Johnson spoke to the public of a Great Society which "rests on abundance and liberty for all. It demands an end to poverty and racial injustice, to which we are totally committed in our time."[216] Similarly, Kennedy used visionary propaganda to promote his New Frontier: "I look forward to an America which commands respect throughout the world not only for its strength but for its civilization as well. And I look forward to a world which will be safe not only for democracy and diversity but also for personal distinction."[217] The supply-side economics ideas of the Reagan administration as well as the '1000 points of light' concept proposed by George Bush were also both supported with visionary propaganda.

Recently, President Clinton painted his own idea of a utopian-like future. In his inaugural address, he argued:

> Thomas Jefferson believed that to preserve the very foundations of our nation we would need dramatic change from time to time...Our democracy must be not only the envy of the world but the engine of our

---

sentence. *See* p. 8-9 of this chapter to examine Kennedy's speech as both symbolic and visionary in its approach.

[215] Warren G. Harding, *Inaugural Addresses of the U.S. Presidents from Washington to Nixon*, 213.

[216] Lyndon B. Johnson, *Contemporary American Voices*, 173.

[217] John F. Kennedy, *Contemporary American Voices*, 166.

own renewal...To renew America we must be bold. We must do what no generation has had to do before. We must invest more in our people -- in their jobs and in their future -- and at the same time cut our massive debt. And we must do so in a world in which we must compete for every opportunity.[218]

In this section, Clinton outlines what must be done for a better future and attempts to elicit a positive response from the public through his use of propaganda.

This chapter has answered the question, "In what manner is propaganda used?" Four different forms of propaganda available to the President have been defined and examined -- symbolic, selective, stereotyping, and visionary. Through these types, the leader may influence individuals in an attempt to alter the A-T level as was discussed in chapter three. The next chapter will answer the question, "What does propaganda hope to accomplish?" It will explore the purpose of propaganda and determine whether the use of propaganda is transforming or transactional in nature.

---

[218] William J. Clinton, *The Election of 1992*, 220.

Chapter Five:

The Purpose of Propaganda

So far, we have examined several aspects of propaganda including its function and its use by the leader. But what is its purpose? What does it hope to accomplish? Why does a leader use propaganda in a certain situation? To answer these questions, I will turn primarily to James MacGregor Burns' notion of transforming and transactional leadership. In the following chapter, his theories will be analyzed and discussed. I will argue that the use of propaganda by a leader can only be transactional in nature and that politics, itself, eliminates the possibility of transforming leadership.

In *Leadership*, James MacGregor Burns recognizes and attempts to address the problems with conventional theories of leadership. These theories usually address leadership in terms of power -- "A has power over B to the extent that he can get B to do something that B would not otherwise do."[219] Burns digressed from the traditional notions of power and generated a "doctrine of leadership with the power and sweep of the old doctrine of authority but now emphasizing the influence of followers on leaders."[220] From this line of thinking two forms of leadership emerged -- transactional and transforming.

---

[219] Robert A. Dahl, "The Concept of Power," in Roderick Bell, David M. Edwards, R. Harrison Wagner, eds., *Political Power: A Reader in Theory and Research*, (New York: Free Press, 1969) 80 found in John Gaventa, *Power and Powerlessness*.

[220] James MacGregor Burns, *Leadership*, (New York: Harper and Row, 1979) 25.

Transactional Leadership

Transactional leadership is viewed by Burns as a give and take relationship between leader and follower. It is governed by cost-benefit analysis. As Burns suggests, "transactional leadership...occurs when one person takes the initiative in making contact with others for the purpose of an exchange of valued things."[221] In The Power to Lead, he expands upon this idea: "transactional leaders, both electoral and media, seek to maximize their economic and psychic income through trading and brokering in a rather restricted arena."[222] The motivation of participants in this style of leadership remains constant. In other words, both leader and follower are fully aware of their desires and pursue those goals. This form of rule encompasses the traditional connotations of power and leadership and, according to Burns, is readily apparent in the legislature.[223]

Examples of transactional leadership in the modern Presidency are plentiful. Franklin Roosevelt used this form of rule to enact many of his New Deal programs. Roosevelt bargained with Congress not to mention interest groups and the American public to pass many of his "alphabet soup" programs. Similarly, President Kennedy used transactional leadership during the Cuban Missile Crisis. His dealings with Khrushchev were geared towards answering the problem at hand. If the Soviet Union had placed missiles in Cuba, "the Kennedy Administration had implicitly

---

[221] Ibid, 19.

[222] James MacGregor Burns, *The Power to Lead*, (New York: Simon and Schuster, 1984) 153.

[223] Burns argues that transactional politics reigns supreme in the legislative branch because of its organization. Politicians depend on the support of local constituents and are, therefore, involved in this bargaining form of politics.

committed itself, in advance, to drastic action."[224] In other words, bargaining between the leaders prevented a possible war. The examples are endless. From Theodore Roosevelt and Howard Taft's anti-trust legislation to Bill Clinton's attempted health care reform, transactional leadership pervades all aspects of the presidency.

Transforming Leadership

A second form of rule incorporates the moral aspects of leadership and transcends the traditional relationships of transactional leadership. As Burns suggests, "transforming leadership...is more potent." He continues:

> The transforming leader recognizes and exploits an existing need or demand of a potential follower. But, beyond that, the transforming leader looks for potential motives in followers, seeks to satisfy higher needs, and engages the full person of the follower. The result of transforming leadership is a relationship of mutual stimulation and elevation that converts followers into leaders and may convert leaders into moral agents.[225]

Transforming leadership, then, involves the modification of both leader and follower. Both are morally transformed and raised to a higher level of moral consciousness through their interaction. Burns even goes as far as to suggest that

---

[224] Bruce Miroff, *Pragmatic Illusions: The Presidential Politics of John F. Kennedy*, (New York: David McKay Company Inc., 1976) 87.
[225] *Leadership*, 4.

transforming leaders "transcend and even seek to reconstruct the political system."[226]

Examples of transforming or transformational leadership can be seen sporadically throughout the modern presidency, but it is more readily apparent through the leadership of those who were not directly constrained by the political system. Both Ghandi and Martin Luther King, Jr. were transforming leaders in that they moved beyond the limits of traditional leader/follower relations and sought higher moral standards in the process. This is not to say that they did not use transactional methods occasionally; i.e., bargaining or forms of persuasion, but that they were primarily transforming-oriented. Burns also suggests that Mao Tse-tung and his revolutionary leadership transformed his adherents through political action.

Does the modern presidency contain instances of transforming leadership? I believe that transforming leadership cannot exist in the modern American political system. Instead, there is only transactional leadership which may consist of either economical or moral goals. To explore these ideas, I will argue that (1) although accurate in the distinction between "give and take" and moral ends in leadership, Burns' fails to recognize the manipulative effects of both styles of rule, and that (2) the nature and structure of the democratic political system precludes the use of transforming leadership.

The Theoretical Basis

Two basic streams of thought coincide with transforming and transactional leadership. Transforming

---

[226] *The Power to Lead*, 16.

leadership mirrors some aspects of Aristotelian politics --
"Aristotle saw politics as a moral activity which required
practical skills and wisdom to be effective."[227] The leader or
statesman acts within a system to bring about the greatest
amount of common good. His or her role becomes "the work
of education"[228] and instruction -- "The statesman uses
rhetoric for persuasion, not to seduce, but to educate."[229]The
state is an outlet for the ruler and its "aim...is the highest
good of man."[230]

Similarly, Max Weber argues that there is a form of
rule which he calls charismatic leadership that involves a
moral element -- "The charismatic leader would most likely
emerge in times of emergency and crisis. His personal
imperatives would be congruent with the social imperatives
of the times."[231] There is, therefore, a cultural aspect to
Weber's concept of leadership. As Robert Eden suggests,
"Weberian leadership stands for devotion to a problem and
task, to an activity as one's cause."[232] Weber also believes
that one of the obligations of the leader "was to teach people
their common underlying interests."[233] In suggesting that
leadership may consist of a moral or charismatic component,
Weber closely resembles the theories of James MacGregor
Burns.[234]

---

[227] Erwin C. Hargrove, "'The Better Angels of Our Nature,' The Moral and
Cultural Dimensions of Political Leadership," *Miller Center Journal*, vol. 2,
Spring 1995, 7.

[228] Aristotle, *Politics*, found in *Aristotle: Selected Works*, 611.

[229] Erwin C. Hargrove, *Miller Center Journal*, 7.

[230] Ibid, 557.

[231] Taken from an unpublished manuscript given to me by Erwin Hargrove.

[232] Robert Eden, *Political Leadership and Nihilism: A Study of Weber and
Nietzsche*, (Tampa: USF Press,1983) 143.

[233] Taken from an unpublished manuscript given to me by Erwin Hargrove. *See
also* David Beetham, *Max Weber and the Theory of Modern Politics*, (London:
George, Allen, and Unwin, Ltd., 1974).

[234] Weber among others also provides a basis for the idea of the cyclic presidency
which both Erwin Hargrove and Michael Nelson, Stephen Skowronek, and
others have discussed. Given the time constraint, I will not explore these cyclical

Machiavelli, on the other hand, can easily be identified with the traditional notions of rule encompassed in transactional leadership. In The Prince, he argues that the leader must be both lion and fox; both strong and clever. He goes on to say that a "prince who wants to keep his authority must learn how not to be good, and use that knowledge, or refrain from using it, as necessity requires."[235] To accomplish his goals, the leader must use rhetoric and bargaining as well as deception and coercion. For Machiavelli, "order is always preferable to chaos,"[236] and through this order, emerges the common good.

Is there a difference in Aristotle's "education," Weber's "instruction," and Machiavelli's deception or are they all forms of manipulation? To explore this question, several things must be examined. First, a suitable definition of manipulation must be formed. Webster's Dictionary defines manipulation as "artful management or control, as by shrewd use of influence." This "artful management or control" can include various forms of persuasion. Robert Dahl makes the distinction between rational and manipulative persuasion. Rational persuasion consists of a revealing of all facts with no desire to deliberately deceive the individual. Manipulative persuasion, on the other hand, "exists when A influences B by communication that intentionally distorts, falsifies, or omits aspects of truth known to A that if made known to B would significantly affect B's decision."[237]

From this line of reasoning, it becomes apparent that there are two types of persuasion based on rational argument.

notions, but I do agree with Machiavelli's notion of historical repetition. *See* Erwin C. Hargrove and Michael Nelson, *Presidents, Politics, and Policy*, (Baltimore: John Hopkins Press, 1984) and Stephen Skowronek, *The Politics Presidents Make*, (Cambridge: Belknap Press, 1993).

[235] *The Prince*, 42.

[236] Erwin C. Hargrove, *Miller Center Journal*, 8.

[237] Robert A. Dahl, Modern Political Analysis, 41

First, there is Dahl's idea of rational persuasion in which A fully discloses all knowledge to B, and B makes up his or her own mind based on the facts presented. Often presidents' meetings with their cabinet officials may involve this style of rational argument. Second, there is the lobbyist form of persuasion in which a rational argument is given to support a certain cause, but only selected facts are presented. The first is a form of persuasion; the latter, a form of manipulation. The difference lies in the deliberate concealing of information in the second type.

Is Aristotle's idea of "education" a kind of manipulation? Throughout The Ethics and The Politics, Aristotle seems to advocate the use of indoctrination for moral means. He argues:

> Nor is it enough, I should think, to receive a right nurture and supervision in youth; we shall also have to practice these things when we are grown men and to become habituated to them, so we shall want laws for that too and generally for our whole life, seeing that most men are obedient to constraint rather than to argument and are swayed by the fear of punishment rather than by love of the beautiful.[238]

In *The Politics*, Aristotle finds it necessary to only instruct others with "such knowledge as does not make the learner mechanical...By mechanical subjects we must understand all arts and studies that make the body, soul, or intellect of freemen unserviceable for the use and exercise of goodness."[239] He limits a viable education to four categories

---

[238] Aristotle, ed. John Burnet, *The Ethics*, taken from *Aristotle on Education*, (Cambridge: University Press, 1967) 96. Similarly, Machiavelli argued that it was better to be feared than loved.

[239] Aristotle, ed. John Burnet, *The Politics, Aristotle on Education*, 108.

-- reading, music, gymnastics, and drawing.[240] Finally, he argues that education should promote the common good and the good of the state:

> Again, since the state as a whole has a single end, it is plain that the education of all must be one and the same, and that the supervision of this education must be public and not private, as it is on the present system, under which everyone looks after his own children privately and gives them any private instruction he think proper. Public training is wanted in all things that are of public interest. Besides, it is wrong for any citizen to think that he belongs to himself.[241]

Aristotle's notion of education is, therefore, not unlike Mussolini's idea of political socialization -- "Anti-individualistic, the Fascist conception of life stresses the importance of the State and accepts the individual only in so far as his interests coincide with those of the State, which stands for the conscience and the universal will of man as a historic entity."[242] This is not to say that Mussolini and Aristotle are advocating the same goals, but merely that Aristotle's idea of education borders on political indoctrination depending on how one interprets his meaning. I would, therefore, argue that Aristotle's selective education which only sees four subjects worthy of study as well as Weber's idea of instruction are both forms of manipulation.

---

[240] Ibid, 109. *See also* Gerard Verbeke, *Moral Education in Aristotle*, (Washington, D.C.: Catholic University of America Press, 1990); and Thomas Davidson, *Aristotle and Ancient Educational Ideals*, (New York: Charles Scribner's Sons, 1905).

[241] Ibid, 106.

[242] Benito Mussolini, *Fascism: Doctrines and Institutions*, found in Dogmas and Dreams, 428.

Although not as blatant or deceptive as lying, it is still "artful management or control."

To return to the original question, is transforming and transactional leadership manipulative? Clearly, transactional leadership involves bargaining and relies heavily of persuasion and other tactics to reach a certain end. The means to reach this goal may be manipulative in nature but may also take the form of "give and take" strategies such as compromise or integrative solutions.[243]Similarly, transforming leadership uses persuasive methods to achieve "moral" ends. It can be done through bargaining or rational persuasion (Ghandi, for example, was a master of persuasive techniques), but it can also involve manipulative methods.

To understand this concept a re-examination of Burns' definition of transforming leadership is useful. The leader "exploits an existing need or demand of a potential follower. But, beyond that, the leader looks for potential motives in followers, seeks to satisfy higher needs, and engages the full person of the follower."[244]This definition implies a form of subtle manipulation similar to that of Aristotle's education, but what is even more interesting is its close resemblance to Jaques Ellul's definition of the purpose of propaganda:

> For propaganda to succeed, it must correspond to a need for propaganda on the individual's part... one cannot reach through propaganda those who do not need what it offers. The propagandee is by no means just an innocent victim. He provokes the psychological action of propaganda, and not merely lends himself to it, but even derives satisfaction from it... It is strictly a sociological phenomenon, in the

---

[243] *See* Dean G. Pruitt and Jeffrey Z. Rubin, *Social Conflict: Escalation, Stalemate, and Settlement*, (New York: Random House, 1986) 140-148.
[244] *Leadership*, 4.

sense that it has its roots and reasons in the need of the group that will sustain it.[245]

Burns is, of course, concentrating on the moral aspects of his idea of transforming leadership, but I believe that the process of bringing about these moral transformations relies on the same methods that are used in transactional politics.[246] Transactional leadership is, therefore, needed to achieve transformational ends or goals.

Burns' concept of transforming leadership involves a leader who not only morally transforms himself but also his followers. Clearly, if I am a leader who has the instrumental goal of reaching or obtaining some moral end, I would be inclined to exchange my thoughts on the subject with my followers and try to convince them of my reasoning. With this moral goal in mind, I would develop my ideas with my constituents, and in turn, would expect their input, and in most cases their acceptance of my ideas because of my moral aspirations.[247] I would have "an eye to exchanging one thing for another," (Burns' definition of transactional leadership).[248] Burns is clearly accurate in his identification of "give and take" or economical and moral ends in the use of leadership, but I argue that these goals are brought into fruition through transactional methods.

---

[245] *Propaganda: The Formation of Men's Attitudes*, 121.

[246] Even Jesus Christ used bargaining and persuasive tactics such as comparison through parables.

[247] It is argued that Lincoln was a transforming leader during the formulation of the Emancipation Proclamation. It is doubtful that if he did have a moral agenda, whether it be to end slavery or reunite the union, that he could readily be swayed by his followers and would expect their support. See J. David Greenstone, *The Lincoln Persuasion: Remaking American Liberalism*, (Princeton: Princeton University Press, 1993). Wilson and the League of Nations is another example. He destroyed his own moral creation through his stubbornness.

[248] *Leadership*, 4.

Democracy and Leadership

In this section, it will be argued that the structure of the modern democracy prevents the emergence of Burn's transforming leader. The pluralist polyarchal system creates (1) a multi-factioned political system which moderates the decision-making process, and (2) because of the structure of the system, the modern presidency must act using incremental measures.

Pluralism and "Institutional Combat"

Although Robert A. Dahl's theories of polyarchy and pluralism will be discussed more thoroughly in the next chapter, an examination of his theories will demonstrate the constraints on the presidency as an institution. Dahl defines polyarchies as "regimes that have been substantially popularized and liberalized, that is, highly inclusive and extensively open to public contestation."[249] In both Democracy and Its Critics and A Preface to Democratic Theory, Dahl explores certain "definitional characteristics" of polyarchy which include elements such as the "right to run for office and free and fair elections."[250] This polyarchal system functions using pluralist methods. In other words, the system is entrenched with various political factions lobbying for power within the system (PACs, interest

---

[249] Robert A. Dahl, *Polyarchy*, (New Haven: Yale University Press, 1971) 8.

[250] *See* Robert A. Dahl, *A Preface to Democratic Theory*, (Chicago: University of Chicago Press, 1956) 84 and Robert A. Dahl, *Democracy and Its Critics*, (New Haven: Yale University Press, 1989) 221.

groups, etc.).[251] To obtain and maintain power, the President must be a skilled coalition builder so that he can maximize the largest quantum of power.

Ginsberg and Shefter argue that it is the deadlock created by bureaucracy, the media, and other political forces which have directly attributed to the decline in importance of electoral politics in America. *In Politics by Other Means*, they outline three trends which "exacerbate the historic fragmentation of the American state,"[252]-- "a system approaching dual sovereignty," "contemporary electoral processes do not provide for political closure," and "bureaucratic agencies have become battlegrounds in, and weapons of, political combat."[253] In suggesting that our system is "approaching dual sovereignty", Ginsberg and Shefter foresee the emergence of a new democratic regime where certain political forces dominate in both the legislative and executive branches and compete with one another, thereby, increasing institutional combat. Whether this theory becomes reality remains to be seen. The 1996 election could place Republican forces atop both Congress and the presidency creating a more propitious environment for policy formation.

The second point involving the decline of electoral politics demonstrates the negative effects of pluralism on the system. Because Presidents depend on the broad support of voters across the nation, they create a frame or matrix of values which apply over a wide variety of topical issues. This framing process allows the President to gain a bastion

---

[251] James Davison Hunter discusses this topic extensively in his book *Culture Wars: The Struggle to Define America*, (New York: Basic Books, 1991).

[252] Benjamin Ginsberg and Martin Shefter, *Politics by Other Means*, (New York: Basic Books,1990) 163.

[253] Ibid, 163.

of support through vagary and the appeal to broad values.[254] However, this support causes moderation of the leader's ideas which leads to the President adopting one of four public policy tactics: "support-shopping, burden-shifting, weapon-forging, [or] political paralysis."[255] As Ginsberg and Shefter argue:

> The political developments of the past twenty years...produce weak and divided governments. Under present circumstances, electoral competition does not create winners with the power to make and implement policies, not does it substantially reduce the losers' opportunities to exercise influence. This absence of political closure exacerbates the historical fragmentation of the American state and leads to a policy-making process that is not well suited to the achievement of collective national purposes.[256]

The political process, therefore, creates many barriers for the President to overcome in his attempts to implement policy. Since the development of the modern Presidency, bureaucratic agencies have increasingly been involved in institutional combat. This has adversely affected their ability to initiate inventive and collaborative agendas and has caused "the destruction of administrative capacity."[257] Although this point may be somewhat exaggerated, Ginsberg and Shefter clearly recognize the obstacles to policy formation.

---

[254] See John H. Aldrich and Thomas Weko, "The Presidency and the Election Campaign: Framing the Choice in 1992," *The Presidency and the Political System*, 251-270.

[255] *Politics by Other Means*, 171.

[256] Ibid, 171.

[257] Ibid, 175.

How, then, does this affect the President and his leadership capacity? The President must counter-balance a number of political factions and inter-governmental conflicts to accomplish his goals while in office. Modern democracy or pluralist polyarchy creates "structural opportunities for wastefulness or for the paralysis of useful state action."[258] To overcome this paralysis, the President must use the "powers available to him...to try to persuade...them that what he wants is what they want."[259] He must, therefore, use transactional methods of bargaining, rhetoric, and propaganda to succeed. The emergence of a transforming leader in this type of system is highly unlikely. This is not to say that a President with transforming goals cannot obtain those ends, but that he is forced to use transactional methods in his approach.

Incrementalism

Another institutional factor which may disrupt the transforming leader involves the use of incrementalism in public policy formation. Because Presidents are constrained by pluralist factions, they are forced to act a step at a time. This "step by step" method usually involves a moderate path of policy formation which seeks to make a move towards or away from a policy chosen by a predecessor. Although it may differ, the policy itself is temperate.

The theory of incrementalism was first conceived by Charles E. Lindblom. In his various works, he defined the concept by suggesting that it was a psychological function

---

[258] Jagdish Bhagwati, "The New Thinking on Development," *Journal of Democracy*, vol. 6, Oct. 1995, 57.
[259] Interview conducted with Richard E. Neustadt, 2:35 P.M., 26 October, 1995.

of humans not unlike Herbert A. Simon's idea of satisficing. He argued that incrementalism was "marked by a mutually supporting set of simplifying and focusing stratagems," such as "greater analytical preoccupation with ills to be remedied that positive goals to be sought" and "a sequence of trials, errors, and revised trials."[260] Other theorists such as Aaron Wildavsky developed incremental notions about the political process. In his book The Politics of the Budgetary Process, Wildavsky argues that "the largest determining factor of the size and content of this year's budget is last year's budget. Most of the budget is a product of previous decisions."[261] Given this, "most debate and attention is focused on the proposed increment."[262]

Through Wildavasky's work on budget reform, neo-incrementalists have been able to merge his notions of "step by step" politics with the theories of policy formation.[263] Michael T. Hayes, in his book *Incrementalism and Public Policy*, discusses the centrifugal force of the status quo. Conservative approaches are the most dominant, and the more radical a policy becomes the more likely it will face a conservative backlash which will moderate its outcome. He further argues that the Constitution and Madisonian elements instilled in our government reinforce "the

[260] Andrew Weiss and Edward Woodhouse, "Reframing Incrementalism: A Constructive Response to the Critics," *Policy Sciences*, Vol. 25, August 1992, 256. See Charles E. Lindblom: "The Science of 'Muddling Through,'" Public Administration Review 19: 79-88; *The Intelligence of Democracy*, (New York: The Free Press, 1965); "Still Muddling, Not Yet Through," *Public Administration Review* 39: 517-526.

[261] Aaron Wildavsky, *The Politics of the Budgetary Process*, (Boston: Little, Brown and Company, 1979) 13.

[262] Robert L. Lineberry, *Government in America: People, Politics, and Policy*, (Boston: Little, Brown and Company, 1980) 453.

[263] Wildavsky has, in fact, altered many of his original ideas in *Budgeting: A Comparative Theory of Budgetary Process. See* Irene Rubin, "Aaron Wildavsky and the Demise of Incrementalism," *Public Administration Review*, Vol. 49, Jan/Feb. 1989 78-81 and "Reframing Incrementalism: A Constructive Response to Critics, *Policy Sciences*, 254-273.

tendencies toward incrementalism that would have been operative under any institutional arrangements."[264]   Hayes does, however, see the possibility of bold policy moves but acknowledges that incrementalism is predominant in pluralist societies.[265]

If policy formation does follow a "step by step" process it would be difficult for Burns' notion of the transforming leader to function effectively in this system. Factions divide and do not unify policy issues. It, therefore, seems unlikely that "power bases" will be "linked not as counterweights but as mutual support for common purpose."[266]   Given the institutional confines of pluralist democracy that a transforming leader must act within, the only feasible recourse would be to use transactional methods (bargaining, rhetoric, and propaganda) to obtain the desired moral ends.

Leadership and Propaganda

In the previous sections, I demonstrated that the modern President is forced to act using transactional methods.   These methods may include the use of various tools such as bargaining or coercion, but the prevalent weapon used in attempting to persuade others is, in fact, propaganda.   In chapter one, propaganda was defined as a methodical attempt to purposely manipulate the values, beliefs, or actions of others.   It must be remembered that this

---

[264] Michael T. Hayes, *Incrementalism and Public Policy*, (New York: Longman, 1992) 8.

[265] Ibid, 6 and Weiss and Woodhouse, 268.

[266] *Leadership*, 20.

is a morally neutral term which concentrates on the psychological aspects that are affected. Because the leader acts within a pluralist democracy, he must as Neustadt argues, have "the power to persuade" which is "the power to bargain."[267]

Propaganda, then, is essential for both the moral and economical ends of transactional leadership. It is used to convince individuals of the proposed policy or course of action. When used to promote moral ends, propaganda exploits an "existing need or demand of a potential follower."[268] It taps into the desires of the masses and fulfills them through rhetorical articulation. The embodiment of these desires may be the instrumental goal of the leader, but moreover, it functions to satisfy the wants of the populace. Moral propaganda, or propaganda that is used for moral ends, uses positive, negative, and satisficing forms of persuasion extensively in its attempt to sway the minds of others -- it manipulates the Anxiety-Tension level. Leaders cannot simply use bargaining or basic rational appeals to convince others but must delve further into the forms of persuasion. In other words, moral rather than economical goals are more dependent on propaganda to be effective because of the increased psychological complexity involved with transforming or identifying with the values of followers. Through the use of propaganda, the President can not only "educate" or "instruct" the individual, but can also establish a common goal with the public; i.e., moral transformation in one form or another. In the past, Presidents have used moral propaganda to convince the public. In chapter four, it was demonstrated that the use of visionary propaganda was utilized for this very purpose. Programs such as the New Deal or Great Society would not

267 Richard E. Neustadt, *Presidential Power*, (New York: John Wiley & Sons, Inc., 1960) 36.
268 *Leadership*, 4.

have succeeded if this form of persuasion had not been so prevalent.

Concomitantly, Presidents use propaganda for economical purposes or the "give and take" politics of Burns' transactional leadership. Everyday usage of this form of persuasion occurs when Presidents relate to their staff or Congressional members. Although it usually involves bargaining of some kind, rhetoric and propaganda often accompany the negotiation. This is not to say that every incidence of communication involves some form of manipulation or deception on the part of the President, but that he is often faced with a situation which requires some sort of propaganda to succeed.[269]

Master or Servant: The Constraints of Propaganda

The modern presidency depends upon transactional methods of leadership, especially propaganda, but the propagandist may be constrained by his utilization of this form of persuasion. First, history limits his use of propaganda. The president is forced to build upon the persuasion he and his predecessors have used in the past. He must act within a matrix which his own use of propaganda has created. If he steps out of this framework, he risks exposing his true intentions and invites public condemnation. The promises politicians make in campaigns are generally remembered by citizens and the media. If these promises are not fulfilled or the politician acts contrary to them, the public will be dissatisfied and question the character and integrity of the individual. George Bush, for

---

[269] The rhetoric contained in the recent election debates evidence the use of manipulative persuasion.

example, in his campaign speeches, argued for "no new taxes;" yet, he raised taxes during his tenure as president resulting in a public outcry.

With the modernization and institutionalization of the presidency, propaganda has increasingly played a more important role in governance. The president must not only be a successful manager, bargainer, and strategist, but must also know how to persuade effectively. His skill and style influence his ability to use propaganda effectively. An adept leader (Franklin Roosevelt) is capable of using a multitude of persuasive tactics to achieve his goals. Moreover, he or she is able to avoid the "backlash" which may result from propaganda.

Because propaganda is a potent weapon, it has the ability to cause a backlash effect -- a second constraint the leader faces in using propaganda. Propaganda is used as the president argues for or against an issue. This propaganda is repeated by the media, the public, and the propagandist himself. Overtime, truth and deception become increasingly difficult to differentiate. The leader may, in fact, begin to believe his own rhetoric. If so, the leader becomes the servant of propaganda rather than its master. The successful propagandist must, therefore, not only know how to use propaganda effectively but also be able to control it. As Jaques Ellul states, the skillful propagandist "must, of course, believe in the cause he serves, but not in his particular argument."[270]

In this chapter, James MacGregor Burns' notion of leadership was discussed in order to answer the question: "What is the purpose of propaganda?" It was shown that the modern president is forced to use transactional methods to obtain either moral or economic ends. This was done through demonstrating the manipulative effects of both

---

[270] *Propaganda: Formation of Men's Attitudes*, 24.

transforming and transactional leadership as well as illustrating the institutional constraints on the president.

The next chapter will examine the use of propaganda within the democratic system. The following questions will be answered: "How does democracy serve the propagandist?", "What psychological needs are addressed through the use of propaganda in a democracy?", and "Does propaganda threaten democracy?"

Chapter Six:

Propaganda and Democracy

Previous chapters have discussed the function, purpose, and uses of propaganda by modern presidents. However, in order to understand the true effects of this form of persuasion, propaganda must be examined within the context of the system itself -- democracy. To accomplish this task, the three theorists (Machiavelli, Lasswell, and Ellul) which have molded the thoughts behind this study will be explored to illustrate the dichotomy in the beliefs about propaganda and democracy. Next, using Robert A. Dahl's concept of the pluralist polyarchy, it will be demonstrated that the democratic regime facilitates the use of propaganda. Finally, it will be argued that propaganda is not destructive to democracy but in fact necessary for the continuance of the system.

Machiavelli: Nihilistic Democracy and the Use of Propaganda

Machiavelli would clearly advocate the use of propaganda in a democracy. It would, however, be used only to promote the leader's own desires or wants. In other words, the utilization of propaganda by a Machiavellian would rarely be used for the good of others or the community as a whole. Machiavelli does believe in the traditional values of democracy as seen with his ideas on republicanism found in The History of Florence and The Discourses. But when combined with his amoral attitudes toward princely rule in The Prince and his discussions of war and leadership in The Art of War, it becomes clear that Machiavelli's notion of democracy would diverge from the traditional institutions associated with the system. Instead a hybrid form of democracy based on the use of persuasion would emerge -- nihilistic democracy.

Nihilistic democracy, as the name implies, is the belief that certain individuals function within the matrix of traditional democracy but disregard any of the values associated with it such as justice or equality. These individuals act solely to promote themselves within the framework to strive for personal success in whatever manifestation it assumes. The Machiavellian individual uses the system not only for his own personal gain, but also acts outside the system if necessary (violence, theft, and other illegal activities). What differentiates the Machiavellian from the average political person is that he or she possesses the potential or willingness to use any means necessary for self-promotion.

Given that self-promotion is the ultimate objective, how are disciples of Machiavelli able to procure this end through nihilistic democracy? Propaganda is the weapon of choice and democracy facilitates its use in two ways. First, it creates a legitimate means for the Machiavellian to pursue economic goals; for, in an egalitarian system, everyone has the opportunity to excel politically if he or she so desires. It is this equality that allows the individual to work within and take advantage of the political system.

Second, democracy provides political symbols for the Machiavellian to manipulate; thereby transforming the state into yet another tool for self-interest and personal gain.

Symbolic propaganda can be used extensively because of the structure of the government. The Machiavellian can also use selective and stereotyping propaganda to manipulate to his own advantage the amalgam of values associated with democracy. How is this accomplished? Machiavelli argues that "men deceive themselves greatly in general terms but not so much in particular details."[271] This is conducive to the use of selective propaganda. The leader can discuss an issue using broad-based generalizations that appeal to values without discussing specifics.

The public is also more likely to frame issues in terms of "good" or "bad", "positive" or "negative." In other words, individuals usually view issues as either black or white and fail to see shades of gray. Stereotyping propaganda can, therefore, be easily utilized because of this bifurcated approach to issues. Because citizens are easily "deceived by a false appearance of good unless they are persuaded otherwise,"[272] the Machiavellian can manipulate others with little effort.

Machiavelli would argue that propaganda is essential in a democracy to help the leader in obtaining his goals. Through propaganda, the leader can move to the top of the power pyramid using image and appearance. One must not possess the qualities necessary to be a good leader but must only appear to have them. Machiavelli implies that the common citizen would base his voting practices on superfluous standards such as gossip, hearsay, or the appearance of the candidate. It is, therefore, the role of the office-seeker to appear only to fit the mold rather than be the ideal politician to win an election.

Propaganda is well-adapted to this atmosphere and also functions as a stabilizing factor in nihilistic democracy. It can be used not only to persuade but to support the system

---

[271] *The Portable Machiavelli*, 266.
[272] *The Portable Machiavelli*, 266.

and its contradictory, altruistic values. In a democracy, one is free to pursue his own self-interests and can in turn use the beliefs of the ideology to persuade others. Through his ideas, Machiavelli demonstrates that democracy is a double-edged sword; that is, democracy, heralded for being a state of freedom and equality which provides resounding benefits to its believers, can also be considered a false consciousness fabrication created by those in power.[273]

Harold Lasswell: Propaganda and Democratic Character

Like Machiavelli, Harold Lasswell views propaganda as a constructive tool in maintaining democratic institutions. However, unlike Machiavelli, he argues that propaganda should be used for education and instruction rather than self-promotion.[274] This use of propaganda in a democracy is very similar to Lenin's idea of the party vanguard or highly-educated group of individuals who would instruct the proletariat on Communist ideals. Similarly, these theorists' notions of the homo politicus superior would consist of the leader standing above politics to morally enlighten the ignorant masses.

---

[273] As Machiavelli suggests, "In human affairs there is one constant problem: in perfecting one thing we always produce another thing that is evil, and the two are so inseparable that one cannot exist without the other." The Portable Machiavelli, 408. Democracy has created a system that honors the individual freedoms and rights of its members but has also left itself open for demagogic rule. Raymond Aron notes that although "one may rely on popular suffrage," it "still does not change the social order, because it does not change the essence of the homo politicus." Raymond Aron, The Opium of the Intellectuals, (New York: W.W. Norton, 1957) 98.

[274] Aristotle, Max Weber, and James MacGregor Burns also advocate this form of instruction.

Where Machiavelli desires maximization of the leader's power through democracy, Lasswell seeks to limit that power. His "ultimate objective is the utter annihilation of that sphere of life and discourse characterized by power."[275] He recognizes that power cannot be eliminated completely, but through the diffusion of control in the "free man's commonwealth," the negative effect of power can be minimized. In order to accomplish this task, Lasswell suggests that the leader uses propaganda to promote democratic beliefs and values.

In The Political Writings, Lasswell describes these beliefs and values as being present within the democratic character. True democrats have "deep confidence in the benevolent potentialities of man."[276] They are also "multi-valued rather than single-valued, and are disposed to share rather than to hoard or to monopolize."[277] They seek to provide citizens with the primary needs of safety, deference, and income as well as the associated values: respect, affection, well-being, enlightenment, and so on. In general, democratic leaders are individuals who desire political office for moral reasons. They believe in the values of democracy and promote them through their power.

Because the masses are "spasmodic, superficial, and ignorant,"[278] the leader must educate the public. Through "goal clarification", the promotion of the democratic character will succeed. In other words, if the propagandist is successful in the construction of symbols and values, then it is possible to limit power and maximize democracy. If, however, the leader uses the system to gain power, a garrison

---

[275] *Essays on the Scientific Study of Politics*, 292.

[276] Harold Lasswell, *The Political Writings*, (Glencoe: The Free Press, 1951) 502.

[277] Ibid, 498.

[278] *World Politics and Personal Insecurity*, 240.

state or other authoritarian developmental construct will emerge.[279]

Propaganda in Lasswell's concept of democracy performs two important functions. First, it provides the glue which holds the system together. It instructs the ignorant public, promotes new democratic ideals, and reinforces existing values. Second, propaganda is used by the leader as a form of persuasion to convince others. The leader may use it as a weapon against external threats as Lasswell discussed in Propaganda Technique in the World War or may use it to maintain or alter the A-T level within individuals. Regardless, of how he or she chooses to use it, propaganda is a potent weapon in the arsenal of tools available to the leader.

Propaganda, thus, can be useful to the leader in a modern democracy. However, both Machiavelli's and Lasswell's use of propaganda runs contrary to the basic tenets behind rule by the people. Machiavelli seeks to obtain and maintain power for the leader and use the system to accomplish this task. His notions of deception and manipulation are antithetical to the many altruistic values which comprise the modern democracy. Along these lines, Lasswell's idea of "concentrating power to diffuse power" also contradicts American notions of individualism and reliance on rule by the people, not instruction by the leader. Both theorists do, however, recognize that propaganda is necessary to buttress the existing system but is it a system worth supporting? Jaques Ellul argues that it is not.

---

[279] *See World Politics and Personal Insecurity* for a discussion on Lasswell's ideas of the developmental construct. *See also* Harold Lasswell, "Sino-Japanese Crisis: The Garrison State versus the Civilian State," *China Quarterly*, Fall 1937, pp.643-649.

The Technocratic Vision of Jaques Ellul

Ellul sees propaganda as an outgrowth of the technological society. The hardships of industrialization necessitate an overarching explanation provided by propaganda. He argues:

> The progress of technology is continuous; propaganda must voice this reality, which is one of man's convictions. All propaganda must play on the fact that the nation will be industrialized, more will be produced, greater progress is imminent, and so on... it must evoke the future, the tomorrows that beckon, precisely because such visions impel the individual to act.[280]

Similarly, Herbert Marcuse argues that there is a visible "trend toward consummation of technological rationality, and intensive efforts to contain this trend within the established institutions."[281]

Ellul approaches modernity using post-Marxist convictions. He believes that technology is the product of capitalism and produces more negative effects than positive ones.[282] Propaganda is the tool of the demagogue who desires only to perpetuate his own power. Ellul sees technology as "the force of expansion of a vigorous society, which is totalitarian in the sense of the integration of the

---

[280] *Propaganda: Formation of Men's Attitudes*, 40-41.

[281] Herbert Marcuse, *One-Dimensional Man*, (Boston: Beacon Press, 1964) 17.

[282] For example, efficiency is considered a basic American goal, but efficiency can also cause a loss in employment. Technology and innovation are still, however considered more important.

individual, and which leads to involuntary behavior."[283] Ellul's concept of propaganda is not unlike brain washing except that he recognizes the symbiotic relationship that occurs between propagandist and propagandee. Propaganda is only effective when the propagandee has a need for it.

Technological propaganda is also easily adapted to the modern climate. Rhetoric based on technology will easily spark interest in the public; for, "everybody is as passionately interested in technology as in politics."[284] Because of that interest, people will be more open to the suggestions of subtle forms of propaganda. Ellul also suggests that "the more one attaches oneself to technology, the more one becomes disinterested in what technology is not."[285] That which is not innovative, efficient, or modern is condemned -- "technology devaluates [sic] everything outside its realm, and renders ephemeral everything that it has not built."[286]

Is propaganda dangerous for democracy? Clearly Ellul believes so. In Propaganda: The Formation of Men's Attitudes, he argues that "private propaganda, even more than governmental propaganda, is importantly linked to democracy. Historically, from the moment a democratic regime establishes itself, propaganda establishes itself alongside it under various forms."[287] It promotes the ideology and attacks other beliefs which are contrary to it. However, in doing so, it may sometimes conceal the truth. As the use of propaganda increases, deception is also likely to increase. According to Ellul, it is this trend of

---

[283] *Propaganda: Formation of Men's Attitudes*, 64. Similarly, Herbert Marcuse states that "the prevailing forms of social control are technological...the technical structure and efficacy of the productive and destructive apparatus has been a major instrumentality for subjecting the population to the established social division of labor throughout the modern period." *One-Dimensional Man*, 9.

[284] Ibid, 49.

[285] The Political Illusion, 64.

[286] Ibid, 64. Italics added for emphasis.

[287] *Propaganda: The Formation of Men's Attitudes*, 232.

manipulating the truth which may be harmful to democracy.[288]

In response to Lasswell's idea of using propaganda to promote democracy, Ellul argues that such a "position is terribly idealistic and neglects the principal condition of the modern world: the primacy of means over ends."[289] Propaganda cannot be used to safeguard democracy just as coercion cannot be used to insure freedom. Ellul continues, "By respecting nuances, he [Lasswell] neglects the major law of propaganda: every assertion must be trenchant and total."[290] Lasswell's idea of democratic propaganda is, therefore, no different than any other form of propaganda.

Ellul believes that propaganda destroys the institutions of democracy and is totalitarian in nature. An individual becomes merely a tool of the politician -- "This is the pure form of servitude: to exist as an instrument, as a thing."[291] Thus, Ellul finds it necessary to eliminate and restrict the use of propaganda in the political sphere. By removing propaganda, individuality could be restored and the institutions of democracy would prevail.

These ideas are, however, also contradictory to democracy. One of the basic tenets of a democratic regime is freedom of speech and expression. Would the restriction on the use of propaganda violate this freedom? Clearly, the evidence against propaganda would not warrant a banning of its use. The so-called destructive tendencies of the form of persuasion have never been proven beyond the abstractness of theoretical research. Eliminating propaganda would, therefore, run counter to a basic democratic institution -- "freedom of expression is democracy; to prevent propaganda is to violate democracy."[292]

---

[288] Ibid, 234.

[289] Ibid, 236.

[290] Ibid, 240.

[291] Herbert Marcuse, *One-Dimensional Man,* (Boston: Beacon Press, 1964) 3

[292] *Propaganda: The Formation of Men's Attitudes,* 237.

Although Ellul does see propaganda as a destructive force in a democracy, he, like Machiavelli and Lasswell, agrees that the values and institutions within the system create an environment conducive to its use. Why is propaganda effective in a democratic regime? How is the leader's use of propaganda influenced by the system? Which institutional factors in democracy facilitate presidential persuasion? To answer these questions, democracy and its values and institutions must be discussed.

What is Democracy?

Democracy, as a form of government, has been defined in various ways. The cornerstone of each definition has been, as Aristotle argues, rule by the "common people."[293] Similarly, John Locke suggests that it was the government's duty to protect "the life, the liberty, health, limb or goods of another."[294] John Stuart Mill argues that a democracy should "provide protection against the tyranny of the political rulers."[295] In the Federalist Papers, James Madison expands on this idea and suggests that republican government should be wary of factional groups or "a number of citizens...adverse to the rights of other citizens or to the permanent and aggregate interests of the community."[296] Regardless of the various values or meanings one associates with democratic rule (liberty, equality, justice, etc.), the basic definition consists of rule by the people.

---

[293] Aristotle, *Politics, Aristotle: Selected Works*, 585.

[294] John Locke, *Two Treatises of Government*, ed. Peter Laslett, (New York: Cambridge University Press, 1988) 271.

[295] John Stuart Mill, *On Liberty*, ed. Gertrude Himmelfarb, (New York: Penguin Books, 1974) 59.

[296] James Madison, Federalist no. 10, *Dogmas and Dreams*, 60.

This definition does not, however, encompass the institutional factors which have created the present American system of a hybrid democracy. To formulate a better understanding of the current political system, an examination of Robert A. Dahl's work on pluralism and polyarchy is necessary.

A Pluralist Polyarchy

Arguably the closest theoretical approximation to the present democratic system, Dahl's ideas on pluralism and polyarchy account for many of the subtle nuances which were previously unaccounted for in other theories of democracy.[297] He argues that modern democracy, as seen in the United States, consists of various factions vying for power within the system. Dahl notes that "Instead of a single center of sovereign power there [are] multiple centers of power, none of which is or can be wholly sovereign."[298] In other words, power is diffused through these various groups giving each faction a certain amount of power but not enough to control the system.

In fact, Dahl argues that pluralism can create various problems in a democracy. First, it destroys the myth of majority rule. In A Preface to Democratic Theory, Dahl states, "that on matters of specific policy the majority rarely rules."[299] Minority factions often obtain their policy goals due to the "passive acquiescence or indifference of a

---

[297] In *A Preface to Democratic Theory*, Dahl argues this notion and points out the inconsistencies in other concepts of democracy such as Madisonian and Populistic democracy. Robert A. Dahl, *A Preface to Democratic Theory*, (Chicago: University of Chicago Press, 1956).

[298] Robert A. Dahl, *Pluralist Democracy in the United States: Conflict and Consent*, (Chicago: Rand McNally & Co., 1967) 24.

[299] *A Preface to Democratic Theory*, 124.

majority of adults or voters."[300]   Second, pluralism "may help to stabilize injustices."[301]   After becoming increasingly organized, "corporate pluralism" may emerge; that is, factions will see themselves as part of the political system and turn towards accommodation rather than dissent.[302] Third, pluralism may "deform civic consciousness."[303] Because minorities are outspoken, their interests usually pervade political debate leaving other concerns behind. Fourth, pluralism "distort[s] the public agenda and alienate[s] final control over the agenda."[304] Given that they are more vocal, factions are more likely to be influential in the policy-making process.[305]

Although Dahl acknowledges that there are problems with pluralism in democracy, he believes that it creates a necessary diffusion of power. This can clearly be seen in his ideas on polyarchy. In *Democracy and Its Critics*, Dahl suggests that there are seven institutions contained in a polyarchy: "elected officials, free and fair elections, inclusive suffrage, right to run for office, freedom of expression, alternative information, and associational autonomy."[306]   This list of institutions mirrors Dahl's definitional characteristics of polyarchy found in *A Preface to Democratic Theory*. One maxim states that during the "post-voting period," "alternatives with the greatest number

[300] Ibid, 133.

[301] Robert A. Dahl, *Dilemmas of Pluralist Democracy: Autonomy vs. Control*, (New Haven: Yale University Press, 1982) 40.

[302] Stein Rokkan, "The Comparative Study of Political Participation," ed. Austin Ranney, *Essays on the Behavioral Study of Politics*, (Urbana: University of Illinois Press, 1962) 105.

[303] *Dilemmas of Pluralist Democracy: Autonomy vs. Control,* 40.

[304] Ibid, 40.

[305] E.E. Schattschneider recognizes the development of pluralist politics and suggests that political parties must "expand the pie." In other words, parties must try to maintain the largest coalition of group interests. E. E. Schattschneider, *The Semi-Sovereign People*, (New York: Holt, Rinehart, and Winston, 1960).

[306] Robert A. Dahl, *Democracy and Its Critics*, (New Haven: Yale University Press, 1989) 221.

of votes displace any alternatives with fewer votes."[307] This corresponds to Dahl's ideas on pluralism; in that, minorities usually obtain a plurality of votes on vested interest issues.

Dahl views the polyarchy as the pluralist modern democracy. He stresses the importance of "a political system that allows for opposition, rivalry, or competition between a government and its opponent."[308] The polyarchy provides for these institutions as well as "mutual security among conflicting groups, a strong and vigorous executive dependent on institutions responsive to a variety of interests and demands, an integrating rather than a fragmentary party system, and representative government at subnational levels."[309]

Given that our present form of government is a pluralist polyarchy, how does propaganda work within the system? Do the institutional factors of the system create an environment conducive for the use of propaganda? Does the multiplicity of values contribute to the effectiveness of manipulation?

Propaganda within the System

Propaganda functions well in a democracy for a variety of reasons. In a democracy, individuals are inculcated with various sociological and ideological values such as the belief in liberty, equality, justice, freedom of speech, freedom of religion, and so on. The number and variety of these values creates a situation in which beliefs overlap one another and create a schema. For example, an individual may place him or herself in the Liberal or

---

[307] *A Preface to Democratic Theory*, 84.

[308] Robert A. Dahl, *Polyarchy*, (New Haven: Yale University Press, 1971) 1.

[309] Ibid, 227.

Conservative schema where one molds decisions on a host of issues based on the label: Liberal or Conservative (a Conservative could be pro-life, pro-capital punishment, against big government, etc.)

Not only do these values sometimes overlap but they may also contradict each other. For example, citizens believe in both liberty and equality as basic tenets of American society, but at some point one value begins to strain the other. Policy makers who seek to maximize either liberty or equality will encounter this tension between the two which often results in increased factional activity.

Michael Thompson, Richard Ellis, and Aaron Wildavsky argue that there are five strands of values pervasive in our culture which act and interact with each other: "hierarchy, egalitarianism, fatalism, individualism, and autonomy."[310] Through their interaction, it is possible for individuals to believe inherent contradictions simultaneously; for example, an individualist can have egalitarian beliefs on certain issues.

By providing more than one mode of thinking, democracy acts as a pressure valve which releases tension, thereby decreasing the A-T level. Propaganda plays a large role in performing this task. It allows the individual to believe in several tenets and values even though they may be inconsistent. How does it do this? Propaganda provides the sub-conscious thought that there are no contradictions. In other words, the individual inherently believes that the system contains all the values and institutions which have been ingrained in the minds of the public.

The sociological and ideological indoctrination one receives beginning with birth has created a Pavlovian response to key terms such as liberty or justice. This is not to say that on a conscious level we do not recognize the

---

[310] Michael Thompson, Richard Ellis, Aaron Wildavsky, *Cultural Theory*, (Boulder: Westview Press, 1990) 3.

discrepancies or fallacies that appear in the system but that the majority of people still believe in the American ideal.[311] Clearly, propaganda is well-suited for a democratic regime because of these overlapping and contradictory values which exist. The president, then, can persuade through the use of propaganda to influence these values.

In chapter two, a distinction was drawn between old and new styles of propaganda. The old form was the blatant, negative, stereotyping methods used especially during war time situations. The new propaganda has developed recently (post World War II) and consists of subtler and manipulative forms of persuasion. Its user directs the psychological aspects of the target audience and influences sub-conscious wants and desires. This new form is especially potent in a democracy. The system itself creates a perfect facade for the user of persuasive tactics. No other political construct offers as many altruistic beliefs which can be distorted and taken advantage of by the clever leader.

Conclusion

Based on the theories of Machiavelli, Lasswell, and Ellul, several conclusions can be drawn about the use of propaganda by the leader in a democracy. First, propaganda is not necessarily detrimental to democracy. Ellul speaks of propaganda as if it were solely manipulation based on fabrications. He does, however, state in Propaganda: The

---

[311] Along these lines, Charles W. Anderson notes that the ideology of democracy "prescribes the aggregation and mobilization of consent as the only legitimate means" of governance. However, "we recognize that possessors of certain power capabilities, control of legitimate force or economic wealth, for example, make or influence policy." In other words, we are aware of this contradiction but continue to participate in the system. Charles W. Anderson, *Politics and Economic Change in Latin America*, (New York: Van Nostrand Co., Inc., 1967) 90.

Formation of Men's Attitudes that "In propaganda, truth pays off."[312] The facts are, therefore, often present, and propaganda generally resembles nothing more than a subtle form of persuasion. The only negative effect of propaganda that is visible involves the ethical questions associated with manipulation. Shawn J. Parry-Giles argues that there is a "rhetorical tension between propaganda and democracy;"[313] that is, democracy, a system based on truth, may be clouded by the use of propaganda. Does this threaten the system?[314] Although propaganda is clearly deceptive, democracy itself is not necessarily threatened; that is, the institutions will continue to exist and constrain the ambitions of the propagandist.[315]

Second, propaganda is needed not only in a democracy but in every existing ideology to perpetuate beliefs in the system. Political symbols must be used continually to emphasize the commonality in shared values. No ideology could exist without this constant bombardment. Propaganda supports the system and as Ellul critically notes:

The individual must not be allowed to recover, to collect himself, to remain untouched by propaganda during any relatively long period, for propaganda is not the touch of

---

[312] Ibid, 53.

[313] Shawn J. Parry-Giles, "The Rhetorical Tension Between Propaganda and Democracy: Blending Competing Conceptions of Ideology and Theory," *Communication Studies*, Summer 1993:117-131.

[314] The tension which results between propaganda and democracy is readily apparent in situations such as the institutionalization of propaganda with George Creel. Similarly, Truman continued peacetime propaganda by allowing the Office of War and Information to function after the war. The Smith-Mundt bill "attempted to reconcile the ideological meaning of propaganda and democracy. Working within the ideological framework of democracy, supporters portrayed propaganda as a discourse that would 'mirror' or 'showcase' the United States in a positive and truthful manner." Shawn J. Parry-Giles, *Communication Studies*, 119.

[315] This topic of systemic constraint will be discussed further in the epilogue.

the magic wand. It is based on slow, constant impregnation.[316]

The vision of the future propaganda provides is extremely important. All ideologies depend on this "strategy from getting from here to there."[317] It places the individual within the context of history. For example, in Lenin's writings, he suggests that after a period he called the "dictatorship of the proletariat," the ultimate form of socialism, communism, would emerge.[318] This prospect provided many with a positive outlook even during times of deprivation. It is easier to deal with present suffering if there is hope for a better future.

The key to understanding propaganda and democracy is to view them as symbiotic in nature. Given this, to argue that propaganda is detrimental to democracy is a moot point -- it is an inseparable part of the system.[319] Elimination, restriction, or regulation of propaganda would also be extremely difficult. The leader and the public must, therefore, assure that democracy continues to be "government for the common good as opposed to government for personal gain."[320] The power of all

---

[316] Ibid, 17.

[317] Nancy Love, *Dogmas and Dreams*, (Chatham: Chatham House Publishers, Inc., 1992) xix.

[318] See Lenin, V.I. *What is to Be Done?* and *The Economic Basis of the Withering Away of the State*, ed. Nancy Love, *Dogmas and Dreams*, 271-300.

[319] Along these lines, Richard E. Neustadt when asked whether he thought persuasion in anyway threatens the democratic system responded: "Persuasion can take forms that are unfortunate for the system. But those are open to others than the President -- members of Congress and the press and leaders of mass movements...No, I don't think this is really negative. Democracy has always depended on warring officials." Richard E. Neustadt, Personal Telephone Interview, 26 Oct. 1995.

[320] Noberto Bobbio, *The Future of Democracy: A Defense of the Rules of the Game*, ed. Richard Bellamy, (Minneapolis: University of Minnesota Press, 1987) 141.

governments ultimately rests with the people, and only through their vigilance, can threats to the system be contained.

Epilogue

Propaganda has always coexisted with politics. It is one of the most pervasive forms of persuasion and infiltrates every aspect of our lives. Every day we are bombarded with propaganda from all directions -- the media, work associates, friends, and family. Because it is continual in nature, the new, modern propaganda remains almost undetected. It creates a world where contradictions go unnoticed, where truth and reality go hand in hand with deception and illusion. Has propaganda created a fabricated world? Are we Marcuse's "one-dimensional man" that cannot see beyond the social order constructed by elites?

Propaganda does have an illusory effect, and if not questioned can lead to blind acceptance of a political or social order, but if placed in an open environment where freedom of speech, assembly, press, etc. exists, then deception will be exposed. As long as the system itself remains open to participation by all parties, the negative effects of propaganda can be counteracted.[321] For this reason, democracy provides the perfect outlet for propaganda. Other systems which fail to offer the freedoms of speech and press (totalitarian or authoritarian) may find it increasingly difficult to escape the loss of truth associated with the utilization of propaganda.

The modernization of the political environment has placed a larger burden on the president who must balance pluralist groups as well as pursue his own agenda. We are

---

[321] This is not unlike Alexander George's idea of multiple advocacy. Alexander L. George, "The Case for Multiple Advocacy in Making Foreign Policy," *The American Political Science Review*, vol. 66: 751-790.

now in an age of the Neustadt president; that is, presidents must rely on the transactional methods of bargaining, rhetoric, and propaganda to accomplish their goals. In chapter three, the function of propaganda was discussed, and it was argued that the president seeks change through altering the anxiety and tension level within the public. This can be done in one of three ways -- positively, decreasing tension; negatively, increasing tension; and satisficingly, maintaining the present tension level.

This psychological appeal reflects the increased complexity with Post World War II politics. The presidency has adapted to fit the demands placed on the institution. Given the scope of the president's tasks, he must get the job done quickly and effectively. To do this, the leader may bypass logical fact-based arguments, for emotive level appeals; for, emotions, not logic, drive many of today's pressing issues. How does the leader alter the anxiety and tension which tap into these emotions?

To accomplish this task, presidents must appeal to sociological or ideological values. Chapter four discussed the types of propaganda which manipulate these values. The president can make a vague appeal to beliefs inherent in our culture or political system (symbolic); he can choose to support one value or group of values over others to incite action (selective); values from one group could be bolstered while others were downplayed (stereotyping); or the president can call upon values not present in our society (visionary). Through these methods, the leader can seek either moral or economic goals (chapter five).

Democracy itself has molded the leader's use of propaganda. With the balkanization of a pluralistic society, propaganda must be turned toward coalition-building. The president must rely on broad-based generalities over specific arguments to appeal to the greatest number of citizens or Congressmen. In chapter six, it was argued that the ideology of democracy necessitates the use of propaganda -- that their relationship is symbiotic in nature. Democracy needs propaganda to propagate its own ideological beliefs and in turn, propaganda is limited by the institutional confines of the democratic system.

What does the future hold for leadership, propaganda, and democracy? Propaganda will be used more as the demands on the presidency increase. There will also be a greater shift away from blatant forms of "old" propaganda towards the subtle and disguised "new" propaganda. Politics has and will become more and more like Neustadt's persuasive leader or Machiavelli's foxlike prince. Image rather than reality will continue to play a greater role in the political sphere.

Has modern day politics become Machiavellian? Many of Machiavelli's teachings have been adopted by twentieth century leaders in one way or another. However, I believe a means/ends distinction is necessary. In the American context, politicians can have a clear-cut idea of goals they wish to accomplish ranging from self-aggrandizement to moral or religious issues. These ends may not be Machiavellian in nature, but the means used to obtain them usually consist of persuasive tactics which he would advocate.

Propaganda is one of these tactics. To say that propaganda is Machiavellian connotes evil or amoral implications, but the fact remains that it is a pervasive part of our society. Propaganda should not be viewed in a negative light. Instead, it should be considered no different than any other talent or ability which is useful to the leader such as physical appearance, intelligence, etc.

Moreover, propaganda is not just a technique used by a leader to achieve a goal, but it is a sociological phenomenon. It exists hand in hand with any ideology and is needed for its perpetuation. It forges the path for modernity by establishing values and beliefs in the present. In other words, propaganda builds on itself. It acts as an ideology's time machine by propelling it into the future. As H.G. Wells suggested: "All human institutions are made of propaganda, are sustained by propaganda and perish when it ceases."[322]

This book is dedicated to Vanderbilt University professors Robert Birkby and George Graham, both of whom have since passed. Professor Graham was instrumental in guiding my research on the theoretical issues while Professor Birkby oversaw this project and guided me over a two-year period. My reason for publishing this book is in part to honor the legacy of their education.

I would also like to thank my wife Alina and son Logan for encouraging me to publish this book. Without their unconditional support, this book would not have been possible.

---

[322] H.G. Wells, *In the Fourth Year: Anticipations of a World Peace,* (New York: MacMillan Co., 1918) 152.

Bibliography

Books:

Aldrich, John H. and Weko, Thomas. "The Presidency and the Election Campaign: Framing the Choice in 1992." *The Presidency and the Political System*, ed. Michael Nelson. Washington D.C.: Congressional Quarterly Press.

Anderson, Charles W. 1967. *Politics and Economic Change in Latin America*. New York: Van Nostrand Co., Inc.

Aron, Raymond. 1957. *The Opium of the Intellectuals*. New York: W.W. Norton.

Aristotle. 1967. *Aristotle on Education*. ed. John Burnet. Cambridge: University Press.

-----. Rhetoric. 1991. *Aristotle: Selected Works*. ed. H.G. Apostle and L.P. Gearson.   Grinnel: The   Peripatetic Press.

-----. Politics. 1991. *Aristotle: Selected Works*. ed. H.G. Apostle and L.P. Gearson.   Grinnel: .The   Peripatetic Press.

-----. Politics. 1988. *Aristotle: Selected Works*. ed. Stephen Everson. New York: Cambridge University Press.

Bailey, F.G. 1988. *Humbuggery and Manipulation: The Art of Leadership*. Ithaca: Cornell University Press.

Barber, James David. 1992. *Presidential Character*. Englewood Cliffs: Prentice Hall.

Baudrillard, Jean. 1994. *The Illusion of the End*. Oxford: Polity Press.

Beetham, David. 1974. *Max Weber and the Theory of Modern Politics*. London: George, Allen, and Unwin, Ltd.

Bellah, Robert N., et al. 1985. *Habits of the Heart*. New York: Harper and Row

Berlin, Isaiah. 1969. *Four Essays on Liberty.* London: Oxford University.

Bernays, Edward L. 1928. *Propaganda*. New York: Horace Liveright.

Bobbio, Noberto. 1987. *The Future of Democracy: A Defense of the Rules of the Game.* ed. Richard Bellamy. Minneapolis: University of Minneapolis.

Bock, Gisela; Skinner, Quentin; and Viroli, Maurizio. 1990. *Machiavelli and Republicanism*. New York: Cambridge University Press.

Boorstin, Daniel J. 1987. *The Image*. New York: Vintage Books.

Burke, John P. 1992. *The Institutional Presidency*. Baltimore: John Hopkins Press.

Burns, James MacGregor. 1978. *Leadership*. London: Harper Torchbooks.

-----. 1956. *Roosevelt: The Lion and the Fox*. New York: Harcourt Brace Jovanovich.

-----. 1984. *The Power to Lead*. New York: Simon and Schuster.

Bush, George. 1991. "Address before a Joint Session of the Congress on the State of the Union, January 29, 1991." *Weekly Compilation*. Washington, D.C.: U.S. Government.

Butler, David and Stokes, David. 1974. *Political Change in Britain: The Evolution of Electoral Change*. New York: St. Martin's Press.

Camp, Roderic Ai. 1993. *Politics in Mexico*. New York: Oxford University Press.

Campbell, Karlyn Kohrs and Jamieson, Kathleen Hall. 1990. *Deeds Done in Words*. Chicago: The University of Chicago Press.

Capaldi, Nicholas. 1987. *The Art of Deception*. Buffalo: Prometheus Books.

Carter, James E. "The President's News Conference of November 28, 1979." *Public Papers of the Presidents of the United States*. Washington, D.C.: U.S. Government.

Coolidge, Calvin. 1974. *Inaugural Addresses of the U.S. Presidents from Washington to Nixon*. Washington, D.C.: U.S. Government.

Combs, James E. and Nimmo, Dan. 1993. *The New Propaganda*. New York: Longman.

Creel, H.G. 1953. *Chinese Thought from Confucius to Mao Tse-tung*. New York; Mentor Books.

Dahl, Robert A. 1989. *Democracy and Its Critics*. New Haven: Yale University Press.

-----. 1982. *Dilemmas of Pluralist Democracy: Autonomy vs. Control*. New Haven: Yale University Press.

-----. 1991. *Modern Political Analysis*. Englewood Cliffs: Prentice Hall.

-----. 1969 "The Concept of Power." *Political Power: A Reader in Theory and Research*. eds. Roderick Bell, David M. Edwards, R. Harrison Wagner. New York: Free Press.

-----. 1971. *Polyarchy*. New Haven: Yale University Press.

-----. 1956. *A Preface to Democratic Theory*. Chicago: University of Chicago Press.

Davidson, Thomas. 1905. *Aristotle and Ancient Educational Ideals*. New York: Charles Scribner's Sons.

De Grazia, Sebastian. 1989. *Machiavelli in Hell*. New York: Vintage Books.

De Tocqueville, Alexis. 1984. *Democracy in America*. ed. Richard Heffner. New York: Mentor Books.

Doob, Leonard W. 1935. *Propaganda: Its Psychology and Technique*. New York: Henry Holt and Co.

Edelman, Murray. 1964. *The Symbolic Uses of Politics*. Urbana: University of Illinois Press.

Eden, Robert. 1983. *Political Leadership and Nihilism: A Study of Weber and Nietzsche*. Tampa: USF Press.

Edwards, George. 1983. *The Public Presidency: The Pursuit of Popular Support*. New York: New York University Press.

Eisenhower, Dwight D. 1957. "Statement by the President Regarding Occurrences at Central High School in Little Rock." *Public Papers of the Presidents of the United States*. Washington, D.C.: U.S. Government.

Ellis, Richard J. 1993. *American Political Cultures*. New York: Oxford University Press.

Ellul, Jaques. 1965. *Propaganda: The Formation of Men's Attitudes*. New York: Alfred A. Knopf.

-----. 1967. *The Political Illusion*. New York: Vintage Books.

-----. 1964. *The Technological Society*. New York: Vintage Books.

-----. 1980. *The Technological System*. New York: Continuum.

-----. 1990. *The Technological Bluff*. Grand Rapids: William B. Eerdmans Publishing Co.

Ford, Gerald. "Remarks on Taking Office, August 9, 1974." *Public Papers of the Presidents of the United States*. Washington, D.C.: U.S. Government.

Fourier, Charles. 1991. *Utopian Socialism*. ed. Nancy Love. Dogmas and Dreams. Chantham: Chantham House Publishers, Inc.

Freud, Sigmund. 1922. *Beyond the Pleasure Principle*. London: The International Psycho-Analytical Press.

-----. 1961. *Civilization and Its Discontents.* New York: W. W. Norton and Co.

-----. 1960. *The Ego and the Id.* New York: W.W. Norton and Co.

-----. 1936. *The Problem of Anxiety.* New York: W.W. Norton and Co.

Fukuyama, Francis. 1992. *The End of History and the Last Man.* New York: Avon Books.

Garver, Eugene. *Machiavelli and the History of Prudence.* Madison: University of Wisconsin Press.

Gaventa, John. 1980. *Power and Powerlessness.* Urbana: The University of Illinois Press.

George, Alexander L. and Juliette L. 1956. *Woodrow Wilson and Colonel House.* New York: John Day.

Gilbert, Felix. "Fortune, Necessity, and Virtue." *The Prince.* ed. Robert M. Adams. New York: W.W. Norton Co., 1992. 150-155.

Ginsberg, Benjamin and Shefter, Martin. 1990. *Politics by Other Means.* New York: Basic Books.

Goldman, Eric F. 1969. *The Tragedy of Lyndon Johnson.* New York: Alfred A. Knopf.

Graham, George J., Jr. "'The Policy Orientation' and the Theoretical Development of Political Science." *Handbook of Political Theory and Political Science.* eds. Edward Bryan

Portis and Mike B. Levy. New York: Greenwood Press, 1988.

Greenstone, J. David. 1993. *The Lincoln Persuasion: Remaking American Liberalism.* Princeton: Princeton University.

Gusfield, Joseph. 1963. *Symbolic Crusade.* Urbana: University of Illinois Press.

Harding, Warren G. 1974. *Inaugural Addresses of the U.S. Presidents from Washington to Nixon.* Washington, D.C.: U.S. Government.

Hargrove, Erwin C. 1966. *Presidential Leadership: Personality and Political Style.* New York: Macmillan Publishing Co.

Hargrove, Erwin C. and Nelson, Michael. 1984. *Presidents, Politics, and Policy.* Baltimore: John Hopkins Press.

Hayes, Michael T. 1992. *Incrementalism and Public Policy.* New York: Longman.

Hitler, Adolf. 1991. *Mein Kampf.* ed. Nancy Love. Dogmas and Dreams. Chatham: Chatham House Publishers, Inc.

Hobbes, Thomas. 1968. *Leviathan.* ed. C.B. MacPherson. New York: Penguin Books.

Hoover, Herbert. "The President's News Conference of October 25, 1929." *Public Papers of the Presidents of the United States.* Washington, D.C.: U.S. Government.

-----. "Statement of Unemployment and Business Conditions March 7, 1930." *Public Papers of the Presidents of the United States.* Washington, D.C.: U.S. Government.

Horowitz, Robert. "Scientific Propaganda." *Essays on the Scientific Study of Politics.* ed. Herbert J. Storing. New York: Holt, Rinehart, and Winston, Inc. 1962.

Hunter, James Davidson. 1991. *Culture Wars: The Struggle to Define America.* New York: Basic Books.

Huntington, Samuel. 1993. "Why International Primacy Matters." ed. Sean M. Lynn-Jones and Steven E. Miller. *The Cold War and After: Prospects for Peace.* Cambridge: MIT Press.

Hyneman, Charles S. 1963. *The Supreme Court on Trial.* New York: Atherton Press.

Institute of Propaganda Analysis. "How to Detect Propaganda." *Propaganda.* New York: New York University Press. 1995.

Ivie, Robert L. 1994. "Declaring a National Emergency: Truman's Rhetorical Crisis and the Great Debate of 1951." ed. Amos Kiewe. *The Modern President and Crisis Rhetoric.* Westport: Praeger.

Johnson, Lyndon Baines. "The Great Society (May 22, 1964)." ed. James R. Andrews and David Zarefsky. *Contemporary American Voices.* New York: Longman, 1992.

-----. "We Shall Overcome (March 15, 1965)." ed. James R. Andrews and David Zarefsky. *Contemporary American*

Voices: Significant Speeches in American History, 1945-Present. New York: Longman, 1992.

Kennedy, John F. "Inaugural Address, April 16, 1961." *Public Papers of the President of the United States.* Washington, D.C.: U.S. Government.

-----. "Amherst College Speech (October 26, 1963)." ed. James R. Andrews and David Zarefsky. *Contemporary American Voices*. New York: Longman, 1992.

Kiewe, Amos. 1994. *The Modern Presidency and Crisis Rhetoric*. Westport: Praeger.

King, Martin Luther, Jr. "I Have a Dream." ed. James R. Andrews and David Zarefsky. *Contemporary American Voices*. New York: Longman, 1992.

Lasch, Christopher. 1979. *The Culture of Narcissism*. New York: Warner Books.

Lasswell, Harold D. 1948. *The Analysis of Political Behavior*. London: K. Paul, Trench, and Trubner.

-----. "Propaganda." *Encyclopedia of Social Sciences*. New York: Macmillan Company. 1934.

-----. 1958. *Politics: Who Gets What, When, How*. Cleveland: Meridian Books.

-----. 1951. *The Political Writings*. Illinois: Glencoe.

-----. 1948. *Power and Personality*. New York: W.W. Norton Co.

-----. 1951. *Propaganda in War and Crisis*. ed. Daniel Lerner. New York: George W. Stewart.

-----. 1927. *Propaganda Technique in the World War*. New York: Adolf A. Knopf.

-----. 1930. *Psychopathology and Politics*. Chicago: University of Chicago Press.

-----. 1935. *World Politics and Personal Insecurity*. New York: Whittlesey House.

Lasswell, Harold D. and Kaplan, Abraham. 1950. *Power and Society: A Framework for Political Inquiry*. New Haven: Yale University Press.

Lasswell, Harold D.; Casey, Ralph D.; and Smith, Bruce Lannes. 1935. *Propaganda and Promotional Activities: An Annotated Bibliography*. Minneapolis: University of Minnesota Press.

Leary, Mark R. 1983. *Understanding Social Anxiety*. Beverly Hills: Sage Publications.

Lee, Alfred M. *How to Understand Propaganda*. New York: Rinehart and Co., Inc.

Lenin, V.I. 1992. *What Is to Be Done*. ed. Nancy Love. Dogmas and Dreams. Chatham: Chatham House Publishers.

Lenin, V.I. 1992. *The Economic Basis of the Withering Away of the State*. ed. Nancy Love. Dogmas and Dreams. Chatham: Chatham House Publishers.

Lienesch, Michael. 1993. *Redeeming America: Piety and Politics in the New Christian Right.* Chapel Hill: UNC Press.

Lineberry, Robert L. 1980. *Government in America: People, Politics, and Policy.* Boston: Little, Brown and Co.

Livinston, William S., Dodd, Lawrence C., and Schott, Richard L. 1979. *The Presidency and the Congress.* Austin: University of Texas Press.

Locke, John. 1988. *Two Treatises on Government.* ed. Peter Laslsett. Cambridge: Cambridge University Press.

Love, Nancy. 1992. *Dogmas and Dreams.* Chatham: Chatham House Publishers, Inc.

Lowi, Theodore J. 1985. *The Personal President: Power Invested, Promise Unfulfilled.* Ithaca: Cornell.

Lyons, Eugene. 1948. *Our Unknown Ex-President: A Portrait of Herbert Hoover.* Garden City: Doubleday.

Machiavelli, Niccolò. 1992. *The Prince.* ed. Robert M. Adams. New York: W.W. Norton and Co.

-----. 1968. *The Prince.* ed. Lester G. Crocker. New York: Washington Square Press, Inc.

-----. 1979. *The Portable Machiavelli.* New York: Penguin Books.

-----. 1990. *The Art of War.* New York: A Da Capo Press.

Madison, James. 1992. *Federalist No. 10*. ed. Nancy Love. Dogmas and Dreams. Chatham: Chatham House Publishers.

Marcuse, Herbert. 1964. *One-Dimensional Man.* Boston: Beacon Press.

Marx, Karl. 1988. *The Communist Manifesto*. New York: W.W. Norton and Co.

Medhurst, Martin J. 1994. *The Modern Presidency and Crisis Rhetoric*. Westport: Praeger.

Meinecke, F. 1957. *Machiavellism: The Doctrine of Raison d'Etat and Its Place in Modern History*. London and New Haven.

Mill, John Stuart. 1974. *On Liberty*. ed. Gertrude Himmelfarb. New York: Penguin Books.

Miroff, Bruce. 1976. *Pragmatic Illusions: The Presidential Politics of John F. Kennedy*. New York: David McKay Company Inc.

Moe, Terry. 1985. *New Directions in American Politics*. New York: Chubb and Peterson.

Morgenthau, Hans J. 1946. *Scientific Man vs. Power Politics*. Chicago: University of Chicago Press.

Murphy, Walter F. 1964. *Elements of Judicial Strategy*. Chicago: University of Chicago Press.

Murray, Robert K. 1973. *The Politics of Normalcy: Governmental Theory and Practice in the Harding-Coolidge Era*. New York: W.W. Norton and Co.

Murty, B.S. 1968. *Propaganda and World Public Order: The Legal Regulation of the Ideological Instrument of Coercion*. New Haven: Yale University Press.

Mussolini, Benito. 1991. *Fascism: Doctrines and Institutions*. ed. Nancy Love. *Dogmas and Dreams*. Chatham: Chatham House Publishers.

Nelson, Michael. 1995. "Evaluating the Presidency." *The Presidency and the Political System*. Washington, D.C.: CQ Press.

Neustadt, Richard E. 1960. *Presidential Power*. New York: John Wiley and Sons, Inc.

Nixon, Richard M. "First Inaugural Address, January 20, 1969." ed. James R. Andrews and David Zarefsky. *Contemporary American Voices*. New York: Longman, 1992.

Plamenatz, John. "In Search of Machiavellian Virtue." *Political Calculus*. Toronto: University of Toronto Press. 1972. 157-178.

Pomper, Gerald M. *The Election of 1992*. Chatham: Chatham House Publishing.

Pruitt, Dean G. and Rubin, Jeffrey Z. 1986. *Social Conflict: Escalation, Stalemate, and Settlement*. New York: Random House.

Ragsdale, Lyn. 1995. "Studying the Presidency: Why Presidents Need Political Scientists." ed. Michael Nelson. *The Presidency and the Political System*. Washington, D.C.: Congressional Quarterly Press.

Reagan, Ronald. "Remarks to the People of Berlin, June 11, 1982." *Public Papers of the Presidents of the United States*. Washington, D.C.: U.S. Government.

Rokkan, Stein. 1962. *Essays on the Behavioral Study of Politics*. ed. Austin Ranney. Urbana: University of Illinois Press.

-----. "Remarks in New York City before the United Nations General Assembly Special Session Devoted to Disarmament, June 17, 1982." *Public Papers of the Presidents of the United States*. Washington, D.C.: U.S. Government.

Roosevelt, Franklin D. "Employment Week and Employment Sunday. Proclamation No. 2331. April 26, 1939." *Public Papers of the Presidents of the United States*. Washington, D.C.: U.S. Government.

-----. "Address to Congress Asking that a State of War Be Declared Between the United States and Japan. December 8, 1941." *Public Papers of the Presidents of the United States*. Washington, D.C.: U.S. Government.

-----. "Message on the State of the Union. January 11, 1944. *Public Papers of the Presidents of the United States.* Washington, D.C.: U.S. Government.

Roosevelt, Theodore. 1904. *Addresses and Messages*. New York: G.P. Putnam's Sons.

Schattschneider, E.E. 1960. *The Semi-Sovereign People*. New York: Holt, Rinehart, and Winston.

Sforza, Count Carlo. 1959. *The Living Thoughts of Machiavelli*. New York: Fawcett Publications.

Simon, Herbert A. 1957. *Models of Man*. London: Chapman and Hall, Ltd.

Simon, Herbert A. 1958. *Organizations*. New York: John Wiley and Sons, Inc.

Skowronek, Stephen. 1993. *The Politics Presidents Make*. Cambridge: Belknap Press.

Smith, Bruce Lannes; Lasswell, Harold D.; and Casey, Ralph D. 1946. *Propaganda, Communication, and Public Opinion*. Princeton: Princeton University Press.

Smith, Craig Allen and Smith, Kathy B. 1994. *The White House Speaks*. Westport: Praeger.

Steinberg, Alfred. 1968. *Sam Johnson's Boy*. New York: Macmillan.

Stokes, Donald. 1992. "Valence Politics." ed. Dennis Kavanagh. *Electoral Politics*. Oxford: Clarendon Press.

Taft, William H. 1909. *Political Issues and Outlooks*. New York: Doubleday Page and Co.

Thompson, Michael; Ellis, Richard, Wildavsky, Aaron. 1990. *Cultural Theory*. Boulder: Westview Press.

Truman, Harry S. "Address Before a Joint Session of the Congress. April 16, 1945." *Public Papers of the Presidents of the United States*. Washington, D.C.: U.S. Government.

Verbecke, Gerard. 1990. *Moral Education in Aristotle.* Washington, D.C.: Catholic University of America Press.

Warren, Harris Gaylord. 1959. *Herbert Hoover and the Great Depression.* New York: W.W. Norton.

Weiten, Wayne. 1992. *Psychology: Themes and Variations.* Pacific Grove: Brooks/Cole   Publishing.

Wells, H.G. 1918. *In the Fourth Year: Anticipation of a World Peace.* New York: MacMillan Co.

Whitfield, J.H. 1947. *Machiavelli.* New York: Blackwell.

Wildavsky, Aaron. 1979. *The Politics of the Budgetary Process.* Boston: Little, Brown and Co.

Wills, Garry. 1988. *Reagan's America.* New York: Penguin Books.

Wilson, Woodrow. 1966. *The State of the Union Messages of the Presidents 1790-1966.* ed. Fred Israel. New York: Chelsea House.

Wittig, Monique. 1991. *One Is Not Born a Woman.* ed. Nancy Love. *Dogmas and Dreams.* Chatham: Chatham House Publishers, Inc.

Articles:

"Asides: Empire's Evilness Affirmed." *Wall Street Journal.* 3 Sep. 1991: A18.

"Changing Sensibilities." *American History*. June 1995: 82.

Bhagwati, Jagdish. "The New Thinking on Development." *Journal of Democracy*. Oct. 1995: 50-63.

Cronin, Thomas E. "On the American Presidency: A Conversation with James MacGregor Burns." *Presidential Studies Quarterly*. vol.16. 1986. 528-542.

Dahl, Robert A. "The Concept of Power." *Behavioral Science*. vol. 2. 1957: 201-205.

George, Alexander L. "The Case for Multiple Advocacy in Making Foreign Policy." *American Political Science Review*. Vol. 66: 751-790.

Hargrove, Erwin C. "'The Better Angels of Our Nature,' The Moral and Cultural Dimensions of Political Leadership." *Miller Center Journal*. Spring 1995: 3-17.

Lasswell, Harold D. "Sino-Japanese Crisis: The Garrison State Versus the Civilian State." *China Quarterly*. Fall 1937. 643-649.

-----. "The Triple-Appeal Principle: A Contribution of Psychoanalysis to Political and Social Science." *American Journal of Sociology*. vol. 37. 1932. 523-538.

Lindblom, Charles E. "The Science of 'Muddling Through.'" *Public Administration Review*. 19: 79-88.

-----. "Still Muddling, Not Yet Through." *Public Administration Review*. 39: 517-526.

Mouw, Calvin and MacKean, Michael. "The Strategic Configuration, Personal Influence, and Presidential

Power in Congress." *The Western Political Quarterly*, Sep. 1992: 579-608.

O'Keefe, Catherine P. "Powers of Persuasion." *Army*. Jan. 1994: 31-32.

Parry-Giles, Shawn J. "The Rhetorical Tension Between Propaganda and Democracy: Blending Competing Conceptions of Ideology and Theory." *Communication Studies*, Summer 1993: 117-131.

Robbins, Kevin. "The War, the Screen, the Crazy Dog and Poor Mankind." *Media Culture and Society*. April 1993: 321-327.

Rubin, Irene. "Aaron Wildavsky and the Demise of Incrementalism." *Public Administration Review*. Jan/Feb 1989: 78-81.

Ryan, Alan. "Do We Overstate the Importance of Leadership?" *The Wilson Quarterly*. Spring 1994: 55-64.

Simon, Herbert A. "Rational Choice and the Structure of the Environment." *Psychological Review*. vol. 63. 1956: 129-138.

Sullivan, Vickie B. "Machiavelli's Momentary 'Machiavellian Moment' A Reconsideration of Pocock's Treatment of the Discourses." *Political Theory*. May 1992: 309-318.

Vizzard, William J. "The Impact of Agenda Conflict on Policy Formulation and Implementation: The Case of Gun Control." *Public Administration Review*. Jul./Aug. 1995: 341-347.

Weiss, Andrew and Woodhouse, Edward. "Reframing Incrementalism: A Constructive Response to the Critics." *Policy Sciences*. Aug. 1992: 255-273.

Other Sources:

Hargrove, Erwin C. Unpublished manuscript.

Neustadt, Richard E. Personal telephone interview. 26 Oct. 1995.

www.ingramcontent.com/pod-product-compliance
Lightning Source LLC
Chambersburg PA
CBHW070142290526
45789CB00002B/588